Mauve Gloves & Madmen,
Clutter & Vine

"So when he was first invited to a Boston party . . . he went with some trepidation and with his resentment tucked into his waistband like a .38." (PAGE 9)

TOM

WOLFE

Mauve Gloves & Madmen,
Clutter & Vine

and other
stories, sketches, and essays

BANTAM BOOKS
New York   Toronto   London   Sydney   Auckland

Mauve Gloves & Madmen, Clutter & Vine

A Bantam Book / published by arrangement with Farrar, Straus & Giroux

PUBLISHING HISTORY

Farrar, Straus & Giroux trade hardcover edition published in November 1976
A selection of Book-of-the-Month Club / January 1977
Condensed in *Book Digest* / March 1997
Bantam mass market edition / October 1977
Bantam trade paperback edition / October 1999

Acknowledgment is made to *The Critic, Esquire, New York
Magazine, New West Magazine, Harper's Magazine* and
Rolling Stone, where some of these writings and illustrations
first appeared.

Bantam Books are published by Bantam Books, a division of Random
House, Inc. Its trademark, consisting of the words "Bantam Books"
and the portrayal of a rooster, is Registered in U.S. Patent and Trademark Office and in other countries. Marca Registrada. Bantam
Books, 1540 Broadway, New York, New York 10036.

PRINTED IN THE UNITED STATES OF AMERICA

FFG   10 9 8 7 6 5 4 3 2 1

Contents

Mauve Gloves & Madmen, Clutter & Vine

Stories and Sketches

"He's a real Mr. Transistors." (PAGE 87)

Mauve Gloves & Madmen,
Clutter & Vine

THE WELL-KNOWN AMERICAN WRITER ... BUT PERHAPS it's best not to say exactly which well-known American writer ... they're a sensitive breed! The most ordinary comments they take personally! And why would the gentleman we're about to surprise be any exception? He's in his apartment, a seven-room apartment on Riverside Drive, on the West Side of Manhattan, in his study, seated at his desk. As we approach from the rear, we notice a bald spot on the crown of his head. It's about the size of a Sunshine Chip-a-Roo cookie, this bald spot, freckled and toasty brown. Gloriously suntanned, in fact. Around this bald spot swirls a corona of dark-brown hair that becomes quite thick by the time it completes its mad Byronic rush down the back over his turtleneck and out to the side in great bushes over his ears. He knows the days of covered ears are numbered, because this particular look has become somewhat *Low Rent*. When he was coming back from his father's funeral, half the salesmen lined up at O'Hare for the commuter flights, in their pajama-striped shirts and diamond-print double-knit suits, had groovy hair much like his. And to think that just six years ago such a hairdo seemed . . . so defiant!

Meeting his sideburns at mid-jowl is the neck of his turtleneck sweater, an authentic Navy turtleneck, and the sweater tucks into his Levi's, which are the authentic Original XX Levi's, the original straight stovepipes made for wearing over boots. He got them in a bona fide cowhand's store in La Porte, Texas, during his trip to Houston to be the keynote speaker in a lecture series on "The American Dream: Myth and Reality." No small part of the latter was a fee of two thousand dollars plus expenses. This outfit, the Navy turtleneck and the double-X Levi's, means work & discipline. *Discipline!* as he says to himself every day. When he puts on these clothes, it means that he intends to write, and do nothing else, for at least four hours. *Discipline,* Mr. Wonderful!

But on the desk in front of him—that's not a manuscript or even the beginnings of one . . . that's *last month's bank statement,* which just arrived in the mail. And those are his canceled checks in a pile on top of it. In that big ledger-style checkbook there (the old-fashioned kind, serious-looking, with no crazy Peter Max designs on the checks) are his check stubs. And those slips of paper in the promiscuous heap are all unpaid bills, and he's taking the nylon cover off his Texas Instruments desk calculator, and he is about to measure the flow, the tide, the mad sluice, the crazy current of the money that pours through his fingers every month and which is now running against him in the most catastrophic manner, like an undertow, a riptide, pulling him under—

—him and this apartment, which cost him $75,000 in 1972; $20,000 cash, which came out of the $25,000 he got as a paperback advance for his fourth book, *Under Uncle's Thumb,* and $536.36 a month in bank-loan payments (on the $55,000 he borrowed) ever since, plus another $390 a month in so-called maintenance, which has steadily increased until it is now $460 a month . . . and although he already knows the answer, the round number, he begins punching the figures into the calculator . . . 536.36 plus . . .

460 . . . times 12 . . . and the calculator keys go *chuck chuck chuck chuck* and the curious little orange numbers, broken up like stencil figures, go trucking across the black path of the display panel at the top of the machine, giving a little orange shudder every time he hits the *plus* button, until there it is, stretching out seven digits long—11956.32—$12,000 a year! One thousand dollars a month—this is what he spends on his apartment alone!—and by May he will have to come up with another $6,000 so he can rent the house on Martha's Vineyard again *chuck chuck chuck chuck* and by September another $6,750—$3,750 to send his daughter, Amy, to Dalton and $3,000 to send his son, Jonathan, to Collegiate (on those marvelous frog-and-cricket evenings up on the Vineyard he and Bill and Julie and Scott and Henry and Herman and Leon and Shelly and the rest, all Media & Lit. people from New York, have discussed why they send their children to private schools, and they have pretty well decided that it is the educational turmoil in the New York public schools that is the problem—the kids just wouldn't be educated!—plus some considerations of their children's personal safety—but—needless to say!—it has nothing to do with the matter of . . . well, *race*) and he punches that in . . . 6750 . . . *chuck chuck chuck chuck* . . . and hits the *plus* button . . . an orange shimmer . . . and beautiful! there's the figure—the three items, the apartment in town, the summer place, and the children's schooling—$24,706.32!—almost $25,000 a year in fixed costs, just for a starter! for lodging and schooling! nothing else included! A grim nut!

It's appalling, and he's drowning, and this is only the beginning of it, just the basic grim nut—and yet in his secret heart he loves these little sessions with the calculator and the checks and the stubs and the bills and the marching orange numbers that stretch on and on . . . into such magnificently huge figures. It's like an electric diagram of his infinitely expanding life, a scoreboard showing the big league he's now in. Far from throwing him into a panic, as they well might, these tote sessions are one of the most satisfying habits he has. A regular vice! Like barbiturates! Calming the heart and slowing the respiration! Because it seems *practical,* going over expenses, his conscience sanctions it as a permissible way to avoid the only thing that can possibly keep him afloat: namely, more writing . . . He's deep into his calculator trance now . . . The orange has him enthralled. Think of it! He has now reached a stage in his life when not only a $1,000-a-month apartment but also a summer house on an island in the Atlantic is an absolute necessity—precisely that, absolute necessity . . . It's appalling!—and yet it's the most inexplicable bliss!—nothing less.

As for the apartment, even at $1,000 a month it is not elegant. Elegance would cost at least twice that. No, his is an apartment of a sort known as West Side Married Intellectual. The rooms are big, the layout is good, but the moldings, cornices, covings, and chair rails seem to be corroding. Actually, they are merely lumpy from too many coats of paint over the decades, and the parquet sections in the floor have dried out and are sprung loose from one another. It has been a long time since this apartment has had an owner who could both meet the down-payment nut *and* have the woodwork stripped and the flooring replaced. The building has a doorman but no elevator man, and on Sundays the door is manned by a janitor in gray khaki work clothes. But what's he supposed to do? He needs seven rooms. His son and daughter now require separate bedrooms. He and his wife require a third one (a third and fourth if the truth be known, but he has had to settle for three). He now needs, not just likes, this study he's in, a workroom that is his exclusively. He now *needs* the dining room, which is a real dining room, not a dogleg off the living room. Even if he is giving only a cocktail party, it is . . . *necessary* that they (one & all) note—however unconsciously—that he *does* have a dining room!

Right here on his desk are the canceled checks that have come in hung over from the cocktail party he gave six weeks ago. They're right in front of him now . . . $209.60 to the florists, Clutter & Vine, for flowers for the hallway, the living room, the dining room, and the study, although part of that, $100, was for a bowl of tightly clustered silk poppies that will become a permanent part of the living-room decor . . . $138.18 to the liquor store (quite a bit was left over, however, meaning that the bar will be stocked for a while) . . . $257.50 to Mauve Gloves & Madmen, the caterers, even though he had chosen some of the cheaper hors d'oeuvres. He also tipped the two butlers $10 each, which made him feel a little foolish later when he learned that one of them was co-owner of Mauve Gloves & Madmen . . . $23.91 to the grocery store for he couldn't remember what . . . $173.95 to the Russian Tea Room for dinner afterward with Henry and Mavis (the guests of honor) and six other stragglers . . . $12.84 for a serving bowl from Bloomingdale's . . . $20 extra to the maid for staying on late . . . and he's chucking all these figures into the calculator *chuck chuck chuck chuck* blink blink blink blink *truck truck truck truck* the slanted orange numbers go trucking and winking across the panel . . . 855.98 . . . $855.98 for a cocktail party!—not even a dinner party!—appalling!—and how slyly sweet . . .

Should he throw in the library stairs as a party expense, too? Perhaps, he thought, if he were honest, he would. The checks were right here: $420 to Lum B. Lee Ltd. for the stairs themselves, and another $95 to the customs broker to get the thing through customs and $45 to the trucker to deliver it, making a total of $560! In any event, they're terrific . . . Mayfair heaven . . . the classic English type, stairs to nowhere, going up in a spiral around a central column, carved in the ancient bamboo style, rising up almost seven feet, so he can reach books on his highest shelf . . . He had had it made extra high by a cabinetmaking firm in Hong Kong, the aforementioned Lum B. Lee . . . Now, if the truth be known, the stairs are the result of a habit he has: he goes around the apartment after giving a party and stands where he saw particular guests standing, people who stuck in his mind, and tries to see what they saw from that position; in other words, how the apartment looked in their eyes. About a year ago he had seen Lenny Johns of the *Times* standing in the doorway of his study and looking in, so afterward, after Lenny and everyone else had gone, he took up the same position and looked in . . . and what he saw did not please him. In fact, it looked sad. Through Lenny John's eyes it must have looked like the basic writer's workroom out of *Writer's Digest:* a plain Danish-style desk (The Door Store) with dowel legs (dowel legs!), a modernistic (modernistic!) metal-and-upholstery office swivel chair, a low-slung (more Modernismus!) couch, a bank of undistinguished-looking file cabinets, a bookcase covering one entire wall but made of plain white-painted boards and using the wall itself as its back. The solution, as he saw it—without going into huge costs—was the library stairs—the stairs to nowhere!—an object indisputably useful and yet with an air of elegant folly!

It was after that same party that his wife had said to him: "Who was that weepy-looking little man you were talking to so much?"

"I don't know who you're talking about."

"The one with the three strands of hair pulled up from the side and draped over his scalp."

He knew she was talking about Johns. And he knew *she* knew Johns's name. She had met him before, on the Vineyard.

Meeting Lenny Johns socially was one of the many dividends of Martha's Vineyard. They have been going there for three summers now, renting a house on a hill in Chilmark . . . until it has become, well, a *necessity!* It's no longer possible to stay in New York over the summer. It's not fair to the children. They shouldn't have to grow up that way. As for himself, he's gotten to know Lenny and Bill and Scott and Julie and Bob and Dick and Jody and Gillian and Frank and Shelly and the rest in a way that wouldn't be possible in New York. But quite aside from all that . . . just that clear sparkling late-August solitude, when you can smell the pine and the sea . . . heading down the piney path from the house on the hill . . . walking two hundred yards across the marshes on the pedestrian dock, just one plank wide, so that you have to keep staring down at it . . . it's hypnotic . . . the board, the marsh grass, your own tread, the sound of the frogs and the crickets . . . and then getting into the rowboat and rowing across the inlet to . . . the *dune* . . . the great swelling dune, with the dune grass waving against the sky on top . . . and then over the lip of it—to the beach! the most pristine white beach in the world! and the open sea . . . all spread out before you—yours! Just that! the sand, the sea, the sky—and solitude! No gates, no lifeguard stands, no concessions, no sprawling multitudes of transistor radios and plaid plastic beach chairs . . .

It is chiefly for these summers on the Vineyard that he has bought a car, a BMW sedan—$7,200—but very lively! It costs him $76 a month to keep it in a garage in the city for nine months of the year, another $684 in all, so that the hard nut for Martha's Vineyard is really $6,684—but it's a necessity, and one sacrifices for necessities. After three years on the Vineyard he feels very possessive about the place, even though he's a renter, and he immediately joined in with the move to publish a protest against "that little Albanian with a pickup truck," as he was (wrongly) called, some character named Zarno or something who had assembled a block of fifty acres on the Vineyard and was going to develop it into 150 building lots—one third of an acre each! (Only dimly did he recall that the house he grew up in, in Chicago, had been on about one fifth of an acre and hadn't seemed terribly hemmed in.) Bill T— wrote a terrific manifesto in which he talked about "these Snopes-like little men with their pickup trucks"—Snopes-like!—and all sorts of people signed it.

This campaign against the developers also brought the New York Media & Lit. people into contact for the first time with the Boston people. Until the Media & Lit. people began going there about ten years before, Martha's Vineyard had always been a Boston resort, "Boston" in the most proper social sense of the word. There wasn't much the Boston people could do about the New York people except not associate with them. When they said "New York people," they no doubt meant "Jews & Others," he figured. So when he was first invited to a Boston party, thanks to his interest in the anti-developers campaign, he went with some trepidation and with his resentment tucked into his waistband like a .38. His mood darkened still more when he arrived in white ducks and an embroidered white cotton shirt, yoke-shouldered and open to the sternum—a little eccentric (actually a harmless sort of shirt known in Arizona as Fruit Western) but perfectly in the mood of standard New York People Seaside Funk—and found that the Boston men, to a man, had on jackets and ties. Not only that, they had on their own tribal colors. The jackets were mostly navy blazers, and the ties were mostly striped ties or ties with little jacquard emblems on them, but the pants had a go-to-hell air: checks and plaids of the loudest possible sort, madras plaids, yellow-on-orange windowpane checks, crazy-quilt plaids, giant houndstooth checks, or else they were a solid airmail red or taxi yellow or some other implausible go-to-hell color. They finished that off with loafers and white crew socks or no socks at all. The pants were their note of Haitian abandon . . . weekends by the sea. At the same time the jackets and ties showed they had not forgotten for a moment where the power came from. He felt desolate. He slipped the loaded resentment out of his waistband and cocked it. And then the most amazing thing happened—

His hostess came up and made a fuss over him! Exactly! She had read *Under Uncle's Thumb!* So had quite a few of the men, infernal pants and all! Lawyers and investment counselors! They were all interested in him! Quite a stream—he hardly had to move from the one spot all evening! And as the sun went down over the ocean, and the alcohol rose, and all of their basted teeth glistened—he could almost see something . . . *presque vu!* . . . a glimmer of the future . . . something he could barely make out . . . a vision in which America's best minds, her intellectuals, found a common ground, a natural unity, with the enlightened segments of her old aristocracy, her old money . . . the two groups bound together by . . . but by what? . . . he could *almost* see it, but not quite . . . it was *presque vu* . . . it was somehow a matter of taste . . . of sensibility . . . of grace, natural grace . . . just as he himself had a natural feel for the best British styles, which were after all the source of the Boston manners . . . What were the library stairs, if they weren't that? What were the Lobb shoes?

For here, now, surfacing to the top of the pile, is the check for $248 to John Lobb & Sons Ltd. Boot Makers—that was the way he wrote it out, Boot Makers, two words, the way it was on their bosky florid London letterhead—$248!—for one pair of shoes!—from England!—handmade! And now, all at once, even as *chuck chuck chuck* he punches it into the calculator, he is swept by a wave of sentiment, of sadness, sweet misery—guilt! Two hundred and forty-eight dollars for a pair of handmade shoes from England . . . He thinks of his father. He wore his first pair of Lobb shoes to his father's funeral. Black cap toes they were, the most formal daytime shoes made, and it was pouring that day in Chicago and his incomparable new shoes from England were caked with mud when he got back to his father's house. He took the shoes off, but then he froze—he couldn't bring himself to remove the mud. His father had come to the United States from Russia as a young man in 1922. He had to go to work at once, and in no time, it seemed, came the Depression, and he struggled through it as a tailor, although in the forties he acquired a dry-cleaning establishment and, later, a second one, plus a diaper-service business and a hotel-linen service. But this brilliant man—oh, how many times had his mother assured him of that!—had had to spend all those years as a tailor. This cultivated man!—more assurances—oh, how many yards of Goethe and Dante had he heard him quote in an accent that gripped the English language like a full nelson! And now his son, the son of this brilliant, cultivated but uneducated and thwarted man—now his son, his son with his education and his literary career, his son who had never had to work with his hands more than half an hour at a stretch in his life—his son had turned up at his funeral in a pair of handmade shoes from England! . . . Well, he let the mud dry on them. He didn't touch them for six months. He didn't even put the shoe trees (another $47) in. Perhaps the goddamned boots would curl up and die.

The number . . . 248 . . . is sitting right up there in slanted orange digits on the face of the calculator. That seems to end the reverie. He doesn't want to continue it just now. He doesn't want to see the 6684 for Martha's Vineyard up there again for a while. He doesn't want to see the seven digits of his debts (counting the ones after the decimal point) glowing in their full, magnificent, intoxicating length. It's time to get serious! *Discipline!* Only one thing will pull him out of all this: work . . . writing . . . and there's no way to put it off any longer. *Discipline,* Mr. Wonderful! This is the most difficult day of all, the day when it falls to his lot to put a piece of paper in the typewriter and start on page 1 of a new book, with that horrible arthritic siege—writing a book!— stretching out ahead of him (a tubercular blue glow, as his mind comprehends it) . . . although it lifts his spirits a bit to know that both *The Atlantic* and *Playboy* have expressed an interest in running chapters as he goes along, and *Penthouse* would pay even more, although he doesn't want it to appear in a one-hand magazine, a household aid, as literary penicillin to help quell the spirochetes oozing from all the virulent vulvas . . . Nevertheless! help is on the way! Hell!—there's not a magazine in America that wouldn't publish something from this book!

So he feeds a sheet of paper into his typewriter, and in the center, one third of the way down from the top, he takes care of the easy part first—the working title, in capital letters:

RECESSION AND REPRESSION

POLICE STATE AMERICA

AND THE SPIRIT OF '76

chapter

II

The Man Who Always Peaked Too Soon

IN 1964 I CAME OUT AGAINST THE WAR IN VIETNAM... AND I STARTED DOING A NITRO AND GELIGNITE NUMBER AND I CALLED FOR THE DESTRUCTION OF THE UNIVERSITIES IN THEIR PRESENT FORM... NOBODY HAILED ME AS A New Left Revolutionary HOWEVER... THEY CALLED ME A NUT. ... I GOT THREE YEARS, SUSPENDED.
THREE YEARS LATER THE SAME THING GOT YOU ON THE COVER OF Time
BUT NOT ME, HOWEVER.

chapter

III

The Truest Sport:
Jousting with Sam and Charlie

DOWN A PERFECTLY GREEN TUNNEL, AS COOL AND QUIET AS you can possibly imagine—no, it's not a tunnel, it's more like a hall of mirrors—but they're not mirrors, those aren't reflections, they're openings, one after another, on and on—just a minute! it's very familiar!—out of this cool green memory comes a steward, a tiny man, in uniform, a white jacket, perfectly starched and folded and creased like an envelope over his crisp little bones. Who doesn't know him! Here comes Bye Borty-bibe—

"Bye borty-bibe!"

He's saying it!

Dowd wakes up and it's 5:45 on the button, as always, and he looks across the stateroom at the steward. The steward is a little Filipino in a white jacket who hesitates, so as to make sure Dowd actually wakes up at bye borty-bibe, as he always pronounces it, and then he disappears down the passageway.

There is something eccentric in the way the day begins. It's terribly genteel!—having a little servant in a white jacket come by and respectfully summon you into consciousness so you can go hang your hide out for human skeet and sweat horribly. More servants will come in after Dowd leaves and make up his bed and clean up the stateroom and dust off the TV and the safe and clean off the desk and take out the laundry. *Only your laundryman knows for sure!* That was the usual joke, but there were some men who came aboard for the first time, and after a couple of hops north they would actually wonder whether it could get so bad— whether a man could get so frightened that he would literally lose control—*only your laundryman knows for sure!*—and whether later, in the bowels of the ship, in the laundry room, there might actually be some little laundry humper, some sweatback, some bye-bye steward of the soul, who would, in fact, *know.*

In the first moments, when you wake up, it's as if you're furiously scanning, painting all the stray trash on the screen, although usually that begins to fade as soon as you're on your feet. In a moment Dowd would be out in the good green passageway. The passageway is a very cool and immaculate green, not luxurious, you understand—in fact, every twenty feet there is a hatchway with a knee-knocker you have to step over, and as you look on and on through these hatchways, one after the other, it's like a hall of mirrors—but it is green and generally pleasing to the nervous system. Actually ... that is not all there is to it. It is also good because, if the truth be known, being on this good green passageway means that you are traveling first-class, sleeping in a stateroom, with only one roommate, and you have the aforesaid servants standing by. It is not even a subject that one thinks about in so many words. And yet the ship is constructed in such an obvious fashion, in layers, that one can't help but know that down below ... they are living in quite another way, in compartments, with thirty to forty souls to a compartment, and they wake up to a loudspeaker and make up their own bunks and run along to a loudspeaker through gray-and-beige tunnels and eat in a gray-and-beige galley off trays with scullion gullies stamped into them, instead of in a wardroom.

A wardroom!—also genteel in its way. Like the rest of them, Dowd is usually doing well if he gets up in time to make it to breakfast with his guy-in-back, Garth Flint, in the smaller wardroom, where they eat cafeteria-style. More than once he hasn't even managed that and has departed with nothing in his gullet but a couple of cups of coffee, notwithstanding all the lectures about the evil consequences this has for your blood-sugar level. But when they come back, Dowd and Flint and the others can enjoy the offerings of a proper wardroom, the formal one. They can take off the reeking zoom-bags, get dressed, sit down at a table with a white tablecloth on it, write out their orders on club slips, after the fashion of a men's club in New York or London, and more little Filipino stewards in white jackets will pick up the orders and serve dinner on china plates. The china has a certain dignity: it's white with a band of blue about the rim and a blue crest in the center. The silverware—now, that's rather nice! It's ornamental and heavy, it has curlicues and a noble gravity, the sort of silverware one used to see in the dining room of the good hotel near the railroad station. So they have dinner on a field of white and silver, while little stewards in white jackets move about the edges. The bulkheads (as the walls are known here) are paneled with walnut rectangles framed with more walnut; not actual wood, which is forbidden because it is inflammable, but similar enough to fool the eye. Off to the side are clusters of lounge chairs upholstered in leather and some acey-deucey tables. Silver and heavy glass wink out of a manly backdrop, rich as burled wood and Manila cigars; for here in the wardrooms of the *Coral Sea* the Navy has done everything that interior decoration and white mess jackets can do to live up to the idea of Officers & Gentlemen, within the natural limits of going to war on the high seas.

The notion often crosses Dowd's mind: *It's like jousting*.

Every day they touch the napkins to their mouths, depart this gently stewarded place, and go forth, observing a checklist of written and unwritten rules of good form, to test their mettle, to go forth to battle, to hang their hides out over the skeet shooters of Hanoi-Haiphong . . . thence to return, after no more than two hours . . . to this linenfold club and its crisp starched white servitors.

One thing it is not good to think about is the fact that it would be even thus on the day when, finally, as has already happened to 799 other American aviators, radar-intercept officers, and helicopter crewmen, your hide is blown out of the sky. That day, too, would begin within this same gentlemanly envelope.

Fliers with premonitions are not healthy people. They are known as accidents waiting to happen. Now, John Dowd and Garth Flint are not given to premonitions, which is fortunate and a good sign; except that it won't make a great deal of difference today, because this is that day.

TO GET UP ON THE FLIGHT DECK OF THE *CORAL SEA,* DOWD AND Flint usually went out through a hatch onto a catwalk. The catwalk hung out over the side of the ship just below the level of the deck. At about midships they climbed a few feet up a ladder and they would be on the deck itself. A simple, if slightly old-fashioned, procedure, and by now second nature—

—but what a marvelous low-volt amusement was available if you were on the *Coral Sea* and you saw another mortal, some visitor, some summer reservist, whoever, make his first excursion out onto that deck. He takes a step out onto the catwalk, and right away the burglar alarm sounds in his central nervous system. Listen, Skipper!—the integrity of the circuit has been violated somewhere! He looks out over the railing of the catwalk, and it might as well be the railing of the goddamned Golden Gate Bridge. It's a sixty-foot drop to the sea below, which is water—but what conceivable difference does that make? From this height the water looks like steel where it picks up reflections of the hull of the carrier, except that it ripples and breaks up into queasy facets—and in fact the horizon itself is pitching up and down . . . The whole freaking Golden Gate Bridge is pitching up and down . . . the big wallowing monster can't hold still . . . Christ, let's get up on the deck, away from the edge—but it's only when he reaches the deck itself and stands with both feet planted flat that the full red alert takes over.

This flight deck—in the movie or the training film the flight deck is a grand piece of gray geometry, perilous, to be sure, but an amazing abstract shape dominating the middle of the ocean as we look down upon it on the screen—and yet, once the newcomer's two feet are on it—geometry—my God, man, this is a . . . skillet! It *heaves,* it moves up and down underneath his feet, it pitches up, it pitches down, as the ship moves into the wind and, therefore, into the waves, and the wind keeps sweeping across, sixty feet up in the air out in the open sea, and there are no railings whatsoever—and no way whatsoever to cry out to another living soul for a helping hand, because on top of everything else the newcomer realizes that his sense of hearing has been *amputated entirely* and his voice is useless. This is a *skillet!*—a frying pan!—a short-order grill!—not gray but black, smeared with skid marks from end to the other and glistening with pools of hydraulic fluid and the occasional jet-fuel slick, all of it still hot, sticky, greasy, runny, virulent from God knows what traumas— still ablaze!—consumed in detonations, explosions, flames, combustion, roars, shrieks, whines, blasts, cyclones, dust storms, horrible shudders, fracturing impacts, all of it taking place out on the very edge of control, if in fact it can be contained at all, which seems extremely doubtful, because the whole scorched skillet is still *heaving* up and down the horizon and little men in screaming red and yellow and purple and green shirts with black Mickey Mouse helmets over their ears are skittering about on the surface as if for their very lives (you've said it now!), clustering about twin-engine F-4 fighter planes like little bees about the queen, rolling them up a stripe toward the catapult slot, which runs through the deck like the slot in the back of a piggy bank, hooking their bellies on to the shuttle that comes up through the slot and then running for cover as the two jet engines go into their shriek and a huge deflection plate rises up behind the plane because it is about to go into its explosion and quite enough gets blown—quite enough!—quite enough gets blown off this heaving grill as it is, and then they explode—both engines explode into full afterburn, 37,000 pounds of force, and a very storm of flame, heat, crazed winds, and a billion blown steely particles—a very storm engulfs the deck, followed by an unbelievable shudder—*kaboom!*—that pounds through the skillet and destroys whatever may be left of the neophyte's vestibular system, and the howling monster is flung up the deck like something out of a red-mad slingshot, and the F-4 is launched, dropping off the lip of the deck tail down with black smoke pouring out of both engines in its furious struggle to gain altitude—and already *another* plane is ready on the *second* catapult and the screams and explosions have started again and the little screaming-yellow men with their Mouseketeer ears are running once more—

—and yet this flaming bazooka assembly line will, in the newcomer's memory, seem orderly, sublimely well controlled, compared to the procedure he will witness as the F-4's, F-8's, A-4's, A-6's return to the ship for what in the engineering stoicisms of the military is known as recovery and arrest. To say that an F-4 is coming back onto this heaving barbecue from out of the sky at a speed of 135 knots ... that may be the truth on paper, but it doesn't begin to get across the idea of what a man sees from the deck itself, because it perhaps creates the notion that the plane is *gliding* in. On the deck one knows different! As the aircraft comes closer and the carrier heaves on into the waves and the plane's speed does *not* diminish—one experiences a neural alarm he has never in his wildest fears imagined before: This is not an *air*plane coming toward me, it's a brick, and it is not *gliding,* it's *falling,* a fifty-thousand-pound brick, headed not for a stripe on

the deck, but for *me*—and with a horrible *smash!* it hits the skillet, and with a blur of momentum as big as a freight train's it hur-
tles toward the far end of the deck—another blinding
storm!—another roar as the pilot pushes the throttle up to full
military power and another smear of rubber screams out over the
skillet—and this is normal!—quite okay!—a wire stretched
across the deck has grabbed the hook on the end of the plane as
it hit the deck tail down, and the smash was the rest of the
twenty-five-ton brute slamming onto the deck, as if tripped up,
so that it is now straining against the wire at full throttle, in case
it hadn't held and the plane had "boltered" off the end of the
deck and had to struggle up into the air again. And already the
Mickey Mouse helmets are running toward their fiery monster . . .

The obvious dangers of the flight deck were the setting, the
backdrop, the mental decor, the emotional scenery against which
all that happened on the carrier was played out, and the aviator
was he who lived in the very eye of the firestorm. This grill was
his scenery. Its terrors rose out of his great moments: the launch
and recovery. For that reason some crewmen liked to check out
the demeanor of the aviators during these events, just as they
might have in the heyday of the chivalric code.

When John Dowd and Garth Flint came out on deck in their
green flight suits, carrying their helmets and their knee-boards,
they were an unmistakable pair. Dowd was the tallest pilot on the
ship, almost six feet five. Six years ago he was captain of the Yale
basketball team. He was so tall, he had to slump his way through
the physicals in order to get into flight training, where six four
was the upper limit. He looked like a basketball player. His face,
his Adam's apple, his shoulders, his elbows—he was a tower of
sharp angles. Flint was Dowd's radar-intercept officer. He was
five eight and rather solidly built. He was not small, but next to
Dowd he looked like a little jockey.

Today they were to go out on a two-ship formation, with
Dowd's roommate, Dick Brent, flying a second F-4B. Dowd's

would be the lead ship; Brent's the wing. The usual monsoon overcast was down within about five hundred feet of the deck. It was another day inside the gray pearl: the ship, a tight circle of the waters of the Gulf of Tonkin around it, a dome of clouds, fog, mist, which was God's great gift to the North Vietnamese.

They climb aboard and Dowd eases the power on to taxi the ship toward the catapult, while the aircraft directors nurse it onto the slot. The catapult officer is out there on the deck with his Mouseketeer ear baffles on and his yellow jersey flapping in the wind. Assuming the preliminary stages have been completed correctly, the catapult officer is supposed to hold up five fingers to show the pilot that all looks good for launch. If the gauges look okay, the pilot then shows that he is ready for his little slide-for-life . . . by saluting. At this point three things are supposed to happen in a very rapid sequence: the catapult officer drops to one knee (to avoid having his head removed by the wing) and throws his hand forward like a cheerleader doing the "locomotive"; the pilot cuts on full afterburn; and a seaman on a catwalk across the deck presses a black rubber button and throws both hands up in the air. This somewhat hopeless-looking gesture says: "It's done! We've fired the catapult! You're on your way! There's no stopping it!"

To Dowd this is another eccentric note. This man who fires the slingshot—or who seems to—actually he's signaling the steam-catapult crew below deck—this man, who appears to flick you into the sky or the sea with his finger, according to how things work out, is some little swabbo making seventy-eight dollars a month or whatever it is. Somehow this fact puts just that much more edge on the demeanor of the pilot's salute, because what that salute says is: "I hereby commit my hide to your miserable care, sir, to you and your sailor with the button and your motherless catapult. I'm a human cannonball, and it's your cannon."

So it is that today, just before he cuts on full afterburn and sets off the full 37,000-pound explosion and consumes the skillet in the firestorm and braces the stick so he won't lose control in the bad lurch of the slingshot, just before the big ride, in the key moment of knightly correctness, Dowd rolls his salute off his helmet with a languid swivel of his wrist, like Adolphe Menjou doffing his hat ... a raffish gesture, you might say, with a roll to it that borders on irony ... but a friendly note all the same ... For this is a good day! They are flying again! There is no bomb load—therefore less weight, therefore an easy launch! ... a good day—otherwise he might have, or would have been entitled to, according to the unwritten and unspoken rules (especially since he has more than one hundred missions behind him)—he might have ended that cool rolling salute by leaving his middle finger sticking up in the air, in an accepted fashion that tells one and all: "You're only giving me the grand goose. Why should I salute? (Here's one for you.)"

But this is a good day!—and Dowd surrenders to the catapult without even an ironic protest, and he feels a tremendous compression, so great that the surface of his eyeballs flattens and his vision blurs, and the F-4B shrieks, and he and Flint hurtle down the stripe and off the bow of the ship, half blind and riding a shrieking beast, into the gray pearl. It couldn't have been a smoother launch; it was absolutely nominal.

DOWD HEADS ON THROUGH THE PEARL, THROUGH THE OVERcast, with Brent's plane about five hundred yards back. The ride to the coast of North Vietnam will take them about twenty minutes. Just how high the cloud cover will be up around Haiphong is impossible to say, which means that the game of high-low may be a trifle too interesting. The weather has been so bad, nobody has been up there. Well ... now somebody's going up there. Already, without any doubt, the Russian trawlers in the gulf have painted the two aircraft on their radar screens. *Painted!* Such a nice word for it! The phosphorescent images come sliding onto the screen, as if a brush were doing it. And with those two delicate little strokes on a Russian radar screen somewhere out there in the muck, the game is on again.

American pilots in Vietnam often ran through their side of the action ahead of time as if it were a movie in the mind . . . trying to picture every landmark on the way to the Red River delta, every razorback green ridge, all that tropical hardscrabble down below, every jut in the coast, every wretched misty snake bend in the Red River, every bridge around Haiphong harbor, every change of course, the angle of every bomb run from the assigned altitude . . . But just try to imagine the enemy's side of it. Try to imagine your own aircraft (encasing your own hide) sliding onto their screens like a ghost stroke (observed by what Russian?) and the trawler signaling the coast and the cannon crews and SAM battalions cranking up in the delta and devising (saying what exactly?) their black trash for the day, which could be inexplicably varied.

One day flying over Haiphong would be "a walk in Haiphong Park," as Dowd would put it. The next day the place would erupt with the wildest storms of ground fire since the bombing of Berlin, Merseburg, and Magdeburg in the Second World War, absolute sheets of 37-millimeter, 57-millimeter, and 85-millimeter cannon fire, plus the SAM's. The antiaircraft cannons now had sights that computed the leads instantly and automatically, and they were more accurate than anything ever dreamed of in the Second World War or the Korean war. But it was the SAM's that were the great equalizer. It was SAM's that made aerial combat in Vietnam something different from what the aces of wars gone by—admirable innocent fellows!—had ever known.

Dowd used to say to himself: "The SAM's come up, and the boys go down." One way or the other! The SAM's, the Russian surface-to-air missiles, were aimed and guided by radar. They climbed at about Mach 3, which was likely to be at least three times as fast as your own ship was going when you heard the warning over your radio ("I have a valid launch!"). The SAM's were not fired at random—each had a radar lock on your aircraft or somebody else's. The only way to evade a SAM was to dive for the deck, i.e., the ground. The SAM's own G-forces were so great they couldn't make the loop and come back down. "The SAM's come up, and the boys go down." And the merriment has just begun. The dive brings you down so low, you are now down into the skeet range of that insidiously well-aimed flak! This, as they say, put you between a rock and a hard place. Sometimes the North Vietnamese also sent up the Mig-21's. But they were canny about it. The Migs went up mainly to harass the bombers, the F-105's, A-4's, and A-6's, to force them to jettison their bomb loads (in order to gain speed to evade the Migs) before they reached the target. But occasionally the F-4's got a chance to tangle with them. What a luxury! How sporting! How nice to have a mere Mig to deal with instead of the accursed SAM's! Of course, you just might have both to contend with at the same time. The North Vietnamese were so SAM-crazy, once in a while they'd fire them up in the middle of a hassle and hit their own planes.

Dowd saw his first SAM last year when he was on a flak-suppression run. Other aviators had always told him they looked like "flying telephone poles," but the only thing he saw at first was a shower of sparks, like the sparks from a Roman candle. That was the rocket tail. And then he could make out the shaft—all of this happening in an instant—and it was, in fact, like a pale-gray telephone pole, moving sideways through the sky as if skidding on its tail, which meant the ship it was after had already dived for the deck and the SAM was trying to overcome its own momentum and make the loop. You were always reassured with the statement, "If you can see it"—meaning a SAM—"you can evade it"—but there were some pilots who were so egotistical they believed that the one they saw was the one that had their name on it. A fatal delusion in many cases!—for the SAM's came up in fans of six or eight, fired from different sites and different angles. "The SAM's come up, and the boys go down"—and Dowd and his whole formation hit the deck and got out of there.

Not long after that, Dowd and Flint were hit by ground fire for the first time—it was to happen four more times—in the same sort of situation. They had just come down out of the dive when they took hits in the port ramp and intake duct. Fortunately it was 14.5-millimeter fire, instead of one of the big cannons, and they made it on back to the ship.

High-low! In what?—ten minutes?—Dowd will have to start playing the same game again this morning. Soon he will have to decide whether to go above the overcast or right on the deck. Above the overcast they will be safe from the gunners, who need visual sightings in order to use their automatic lead mechanisms. But right above the overcast is where SAM rules like a snake. More aviators have been wiped out by SAM's popping out of the clouds they're sitting on than any other way. Rather than contend with that automated blind beast, some pilots prefer to come in low over the terrain in the eternal attempt to get in "under the radar." But what is it really, a strategic defense or a psychological defense?

Such was the nature of the game that Dowd and every other pilot here had to play. Many of the pilots who flew over Vietnam had been trained by instructors who had flown in the Korean war. What tigers those old Korea jocks were! What glorious memories they had! What visions those aces could fill your skull with! What a tangy taste they gave to the idea of aerial combat over Southeast Asia! The Korean war brought on the first air-to-air combat between jet fighters, but it turned out to be dogfighting of the conventional sort nonetheless, American F-86's versus Soviet-built Mig-15's mainly—and it was a picnic . . . a field day . . . a duck shoot . . . American pilots, flying F-86's in all but a few dozen cases, shot down 839 Korean and Chinese Mig-15's. Only fifty-six F-86's were lost. Quite a carnival it was. Morale among American ground troops in Korea slid like the mud, but the pilots were in Fighter Jock Heaven. The Air Force was producing aces—fighter pilots who had shot down five planes or more—as fast as the Communists could get the Migs up in the air. By the time the war stopped, there were thirty-eight Air Force aces, and between them they had accounted for a total of 299.5 kills. High spirits these lads had. They chronicled their adventures with a good creamy romanticism such as nobody in flying had dared treat himself to since the days of Lufbery, Frank Luke, and Von Richthofen in the First World War. Why hold back! Jousting is jousting, and a knight's a knight. Colonel Harrison R. Thyng, who shot down five Migs in Korea (and eight German and Japanese planes in the Second World War), glowed like Excalibur when he described his Fourth Fighter-Interceptor Wing: "Like olden knights the F-86 pilots ride up over North Korea to the Yalu River, the sun glinting off silver aircraft, contrails streaming behind, as they challenge the numerically superior enemy to come on up and fight." Lances and plumes! Come on up and fight! Now there was a man having a wonderful time!

In Vietnam, however, the jousting was of a kind the good colonel and his knights never dreamed of. The fighter plane that the Air Force and the Navy were now using instead of the F-86—namely, the F-4—was competing with the new generation of Migs and was winning by a ratio of two to one, according to the air-to-air combat scoreboards, regular league standings, that were kept in various military publications. That was nothing like the fifteen-to-one ratio in Korea, of course—but more than that, it was not even the main event any longer. Not even the heroic word "ace" carried the old wallop. The studs-of-all-the-studs in Vietnam were not the pilots in air-to-air combat but the men who operated in that evil space between the rock and the hard place, between the SAM's and the automatic cannon fire.

In the past three years—1965, 1966, and the year just ending for John Dowd, 1967—the losses had been more brutal than the Air Force or the Navy had ever admitted. Jack Broughton, an Air Force colonel and commander of a wing of F-105's flying over Hanoi-Haiphong from out of Thailand, described the losses as "astronomical and unacceptable," and they were increasing sharply each year. What made the North Vietnamese game of high-low—SAM's and ground fire—so effective was a set of restrictions such as no combat pilots had ever had to contend with before.

Flying out over Hanoi and Haiphong was like playing on some small and sharply defined court. These two cities were by far the major targets in North Vietnam, and so there was very little element of surprise along the lines of switching targets. They could only be approached down a ridge of mountains ("Thud Ridge") from the west, out of Thailand, which would be the Air Force attacking with F-105 fighter-bombers, or across a wide-open delta (perfect for radar defenses) from the east, which would be the Navy attacking from carriers in the gulf. The North Vietnamese and the Russians packed so much artillery in and around these two cities that pilots would come back saying, "It was like trying to fly through a rainstorm without hitting a drop."

God knows how many planes and pilots were lost just trying to knock out the North Vietnamese ground fire. The Air Force had Wild Weasel or Iron Hand units made up of pilots in F-105's who offered themselves as living SAM bait. They would deliberately try to provoke launches by the SAM battalions so that other ships could get a radar lock on the SAM sites and hit them with cluster-bomb strikes. This became the ultimate game of radar chess. If the SAM battalions beamed up at the Wild Weasels and committed too early, they stood to get obliterated, which would also allow the main strike force to get through to its target. On the other hand, if they refused to go for the bait, recognizing it for what it was, and shut down their beams—that might give the strike force just enough time to slip through unchallenged. So they'd keep shutting on and off, as in some lethal game of "one finger, two fingers." Their risk was nothing, however, compared to that of the Wild Weasel pilots, who were the first in and the last out, who hung around in the evil space far too long and stood to get snuffed any way the game went.

Navy pilots, Dowd among them, were sent out day after day

for "flak suppression." The North Vietnamese could move their flak sites around overnight, so that the only way to find them was by leading with your head, as it were, flying over the target area until you saw them fire the cannons. This you could detect by the rather pretty peach-pink sparkles, which were the muzzle explosions. The cannons made no sound at all (way up here) and seemed tiny and merely decorative . . . with their little delicate peach-pink sparkles amid the bitter green of the scrabble. Dowd and his comrades could not unload on these flak sites just anywhere they found them, however. As if to make the game a little more hazardous, the Pentagon had declared certain areas bomb-free zones. A pilot could hit only "military targets," which meant he couldn't hit villages, hospitals, churches, or Haiphong harbor if there was a "third-party" ship there. So, naturally, being no fools, the North Vietnamese loaded the villages up with flak sites, loaded the churches up with munitions, put SAM sites behind the hospitals, and "welded a third-party ship to the dock" in Haiphong harbor, as Garth Flint put it. There always seemed to be some neutral flag in port there, with one of North Vietnam's best customers being our friends the British. One day one of Dowd's *Coral Sea* comrades came in for a run on a railroad freight depot, pickled his bombs too soon, went long, and hit a church—whereupon the bitter-green landscape rocked with secondary and tertiary explosions and a succession of fireballs. The place had gone up like an arsenal, which of course it was. Every now and then Dowd would be involved in a strike aimed at "cutting off" Haiphong harbor. This was not to be done, however, by mining the harbor or blowing the docking facilities out of the water or in any other obvious and easy manner. No, this had to be accomplished by surgically severing the bridges that connected the port with the mainland. This required bomb runs through the eye of a needle, and even if the bridges were knocked out, the North Vietnamese simply moved everything across by barge until the bridges were back.

If you were a pilot being flung out every day between the rock and the hard place, these complicated proscriptions took on an eerie diffidence, finally. They were like an unaccountable display of delicate manners. In fact, it was the Johnson Administration's attempt to fight a "humane" war and look good in the eyes of the world. There was something out-to-lunch about it, however. The eyes of the world did not flutter for a second. Stories of American atrocities were believed by whoever wanted to believe them, no matter what actually occurred, and the lacy patterns that American bombing missions had to follow across Hanoi-Haiphong never impressed a soul, except for the pilots and radar-intercept officers who knew what a difficult and dangerous game it was.

If the United States was seriously trying to win the battle of world opinion—well, then, here you had a real bush-league operation. The North Vietnamese were the uncontested aces, once you got into this arena. One of the most galling things a pilot had to endure in Vietnam was seeing the North Vietnamese pull propaganda coup after propaganda coup, often with the help, unwitting or otherwise, of Americans. There was not merely a sense of humiliation about it. The North Vietnamese talent in this direction often had direct strategic results.

For example, the missions over N—— D——. Now, here was one time, in Dowd's estimation, when they had gotten the go-ahead to do the job right. N—— D—— was an important transportation center in the Iron Triangle area. For two days they softened the place up, working on the flak sites and SAM sites in the most methodical way. On the third day they massed the bomb strike itself. They tore the place apart. They ripped open its gullet. They put it out of the transport business. It had been a model operation. But the North Vietnamese now are blessed with a weapon that no military device known to America could ever get a lock on. As if by magic . . . in Hanoi . . . appears . . . Harrison Salisbury! Harrison Salisbury—writing in *The New York Times* about the atrocious American bombing of the hardscrabble folk of North Vietnam in the Iron Triangle! If you had real sporting blood in you, you had to hand it to the North Vietnamese. They were champions at this sort of thing. It was beautiful to watch. To Americans who knew the air war in the north firsthand, it seemed as if the North Vietnamese were playing Mr. Harrison Salisbury of *The New York Times* like an ocarina, as if they were blowing smoke up his pipe and the finger work was just right and the song was coming forth better than they could have played it themselves.

Before you knew it, massive operations like the one at N—— D—— were no longer being carried out. It was back to threading needles. And yet it couldn't simply be blamed on Salisbury. No series of articles by anyone, no matter what the publication, could have had such an immediate strategic effect if there weren't some sort of strange collapse of will power taking place back in the States. One night, after a couple of hops, Dowd sank back into an easy chair in the wardroom of the *Coral Sea* and picked up a copy of some newspaper that was lying around. There on the first page was William Sloane Coffin, the Yale University chaplain, leading a student antiwar protest. Not only that, there was Kingman Brewster, the president of Yale, standing by, offering tacit support . . . or at least not demurring in any way. It gave Dowd a very strange feeling. Out in the Gulf of Tonkin, on a carrier, one was not engulfed in news from stateside. A report like this came like a remote slice of something—but a slice of something how big? Coffin, who had been at Yale when Dowd was there—Coffin was one thing. But the president of Yale? There was Kingman Brewster with his square-cut face—but looked at another way, it was a strong face gone flaccid, plump as a piece of chicken Kiev. Six years before, when Dowd was a senior at Yale and had his picture taken on the Yale Fence as captain of the basketball team . . . any such Yale scene as was now in this newspaper would have been impossible to contemplate.

The collapse of morale, or weakening of resolve, or whatever it should be called—this was all taking place in the States at the very moment when the losses were beginning to mount in both the Navy and the Air Force. Aviators were getting shot down by the hundreds. Sometimes, at night, after dinner, after the little stewards in white had cleared away the last of the silver from off the white line, after playing a few rounds of acey-deucey in the lounge or just sinking into the leather billows of the easy chairs, after a movie in the wardroom, after a couple of unauthorized but unofficially tolerated whiskeys in somebody's stateroom—after the usual, in short, when he was back in his own quarters, Dowd would take out his mimeographed flight schedule for the day just completed and turn it over to the blank side and use it to keep a journal. In 1966 and 1967 more and more of these entries would make terse note of the toll of friends: "We lost Paul Schultz & Sully—presumably captured immediately on landing in parachute. Direct hit from SAM coming out of clouds—site near Kien An." Or: "Bill C. got it over Ha Tinh today—body seen bloody on ground."

Or they were about how John Dowd hadn't gotten his: "The Lord giveth and the Lord taketh away. I think today was a *give* day. 8 SAM's or so fired from multiple sites and it looked like a few had my no. on them. However they missed their mark & so this entry is made . . . Doc H. presented those who participated in the 'A' strike with a little vial of J. W. Dant cough medicine."

IN LIGHT OF ALL THAT, IT MAY BE OF INTEREST TO NOTE ONE fact concerning the mission to Haiphong and points north that Dowd has just headed off on: he did not merely volunteer for it—he thought it up!

For four days, which is to say, ever since Christmas Day, the coastal ports of Haiphong, Cam Pha, and Hon Gay have been socked in with bad weather. Dowd suggested and volunteered for a weather-reconnaissance hop to find out how bad it actually was, to see if the soup was moving at all, to see if the harbors were by any chance clear of third-party ships and therefore eligible for bombing, and so on. If anyone had asked, Dowd would have merely said that anything was better than sitting around the ship for days on end, doing make-work.

But *any*thing—even playing high-low with SAM over the North?

The answer to that question perhaps leads to the answer to a broader one: How was it that despite their own fearsome losses in 1965, 1966 and 1967, despite hobbling restrictions and dubious strategies set by the Pentagon, despite the spectacle of the antiwar movement building back home—how was it that, in the face of all this, American fliers in Vietnam persisted in virtuoso performances and amazing displays of *esprit* throughout the war? Somehow it got down to something that is encoded in the phrase "a great hop."

The last time Dowd and Garth Flint were out was four days ago, Christmas Day, during the American Christmas cease-fire; and what a little tourist excursion that was. They flew a photo run over Route IA in North Vietnam, came in under the cloud cover, right down on top of the "Drive-In," as it was called, fifty feet from the ground, with Garth taking pictures, and the Charlies were down there using Christmas Day and the cease-fire for all it was worth. The traffic jam at the Phun Cat ferry, going south to the Ho Chi Minh Trail, was so enormous that they couldn't have budged even if they thought Dowd was going to open up on them. They craned their heads back and stared up at him. He was down so low, it was as if he could have chucked them under their chins. Several old geezers, in the inevitable pantaloons, looked up without even taking their hands off the drafts of the wagons they were pulling. It was as if they were harnessed to them. The wagons were so full of artillery shells, it was hard to see how one man, particularly so spindly a creature, could possibly pull one, but there they were in the middle of the general jam-up, in with the trucks, bicycles, motorcycles, old cars, rigs of every sort, anything that would roll.

Now, that was a good hop—and Dowd so recorded it in his

journal—an interesting hop, a nice slice of the war, something to talk about, but merely a photo hop . . . and not *a great hop*. There was such a thing as a great hop, and it was quite something else.

Sometimes, at night, when Dowd would write on the back of his flight schedule, he'd make such entries as:

"Great hop! Went to Nam Dinh and hosed down the flak sites around that city. Migs joined in the caper, but no one got a tally. Think I lucked out in a last-minute bomb run & racked up a flak site pretty well."

The atmosphere of the great hop had something about it that was *warlike* only in the sense that it was, literally, a part of combat. A word that comes closer is *sporting*. Throughout his tour of duty on the *Coral Sea,* no matter how bearish the missions became, Dowd seemed to maintain an almost athletic regard for form. Even on days he spent diving from SAM's and running the flak gauntlets, even on days when he was hit by flak, he would wind up his journal entries with a note about how well (or how poorly) he drove his F-4 back down onto the carrier, and often with a playful tone: "2nd pass was a beauty but only received an OK—which was an unfortunate misjudgment on the part of the LSO [landing signal officer]." Or: "Went to Haiphong Barracks. 3 SAM's launched—one appeared to be directed at yours truly— however with skill & cunning we managed to avoid it, although it cost us our first bombing run, which was in question due to lack of a target—no flak to suppress. After whifferdilling around we rolled in on a preplanned secondary target. What deleterious havoc this bombing caused the enemy is questionable. However the overall mission was quite successful . . . RTB good approach except for last ¼ mile. Received *cut-1* for my efforts."

A great hop! *With skill & cunning we managed to avoid . . .* death, to call it by its right name. But pilots never mentioned death in the abstract. In fact, the word itself was taboo in conversation. So were the words "bravery" and "fear" and their synonyms. Which is to say, pilots never mentioned the three questions that were uppermost in the minds of all of them: Will I live or die? Will I be brave, whatever happens? Will I show my fear? By now, 1967, with more than a hundred combat missions behind him, Dowd existed in a mental atmosphere that was very nearly mystical. Pilots who had survived that many games of high-low over North Vietnam were like the preacher in *Moby Dick* who ascends to the pulpit on a rope ladder and then pulls the ladder up behind him.

Friends, near ones and dear ones, the loved ones back home, often wondered just what was on the minds of the fliers as the casualties began to increase at a fearsome rate in 1966 and 1967. Does a flier lie on his back in bed at night with his eyes wide open, staring holes through the ceiling and the flight deck and into outer space, thinking of the little ones, Jeffrey and Jennifer, or of his wife, Sandy, and of the soft lost look she has when she first wakes in the morning or of Mom and Dad and Christmas and of little things like how he used to click the toggles on his rubber boots into place before he went out into the snow when he was eight? No, my dear ones back home—I'm afraid not! The lads did not lie in their staterooms on the *Coral Sea* thinking of these things—not even on Christmas Eve, a few days ago!

Well . . . what was on their minds?

(Hmmmm . . . How to put it into words . . . Should it be called the "inner room"?)

Dowd, for one, had entered the Navy in 1961 without the slightest thought of flying or of going to war. The Navy had no such designs for him, either. Quite the contrary. All they asked was that he keep playing basketball! At Yale, Dowd had been an aggressive player, the sort who was matched up against other college stars, such as Dave De Busschere of the University of Detroit (later of the New York Knicks). At the end of his last season, 1961, Dowd was drafted by the Cleveland entry in the new American Basketball Association. He had his naval R.O.T.C. obligation to serve out, however, and the Navy sent him to Hawaii to play ball for the fleet. This he did; his team won the All-Navy champi-

onship in 1962. There was nothing to stop him from playing basketball for the rest of his service stint . . . just putting the ball in
the hoop for Uncle Sam in heavy-lidded Hawaii.

Now that he was in the military, however, Dowd, like many
service athletes, began to get a funny feeling. It had to do with the
intangible thing that made sports so alluring when you were in
school or college, the intangible summed up in the phrase "where
the action is." At Yale, as at other colleges, playing sports was
where the action was—or where the applause, the stardom, and
the honor were, to be more exact. But now that he was in the
Navy, something about sports, something he had never thought
about, became obvious. Namely, all team sports were play-acting
versions of military combat.

It is no mere coincidence that the college sport where there is
the greatest risk of injury—football—is also the most prestigious.
But the very risk of injury in football is itself but a mild play-
acting version of the real thing: the risk of death in military action. So a service athlete was like a dilettante. He was play-acting
inside the arena of the real thing. The real thing was always
available, any time one had the stomach for it, even in peacetime.
There were plenty of ways to hang your side out over the edge in
the service, even without going to war. Quite unconsciously, the
service athlete always felt mocked by that unspoken challenge.
And in the Navy there was no question but that *the* action-of-all-
actions was flying fighter planes off carriers.

In his last year at Yale, Dowd had married a girl named
Wendy Harter from his home town, Rockville Centre, Long Island. About a year and a half later they had a son, John Jr. And
then, out in Hawaii, on those hot liquid evenings when the boy
couldn't go to sleep, they would drive him out to Hickam Field
to watch the airplanes. Both commercial liners and military
fighters came into Hickam. By and by Dowd was taking his wife
and his son out there even when the boy was practically asleep in
his tracks. One night they were out at Hickam, and Wendy surprised Dowd by reading his mind out loud for him.

"If you like them so much," she said, "why don't you fly them?"

So he started training . . . with a vague feeling of *pour le sport*. This was 1963, when the possibility of an American war in Vietnam was not even talked about.

A man may go into military flight training believing that he is entering some sort of technical school where he is simply going to acquire a certain set of skills. Instead, he finds himself enclosed in the walls of a fraternity. That was the first big surprise for every student. Flying was not a craft but a fraternity. Not only that, the activities of this particular brotherhood began to consume all of a man's waking hours.

But why? And why was it so obsessive? Ahhhhh—*we don't talk about that!* Nevertheless, the explanation was: flying required not merely talent but one of the grandest gambles of manhood. Flying, particularly in the military, involved an abnormal risk of death at every stage. Being a military flight instructor was a more hazardous occupation than deep-sea diving. For that matter, simply taking off in a single-engine jet fighter, such as an F-102, or any other of the military's marvelous bricks with fins on them, presented a man, on a perfectly sunny day, with more ways to get himself killed than his wife and children could possibly imagine. Within the fraternity of men who did this sort of thing day in and day out—within the flying fraternity, that is—mankind appeared to be sheerly divided into those who have it and those who don't—although just what *it* was . . . was never explained. Moreover, the very subject was taboo. *It* somehow seemed to be the transcendent solution to the binary problem of Death/Glory, but since not even the *terminology* could be uttered, speculating on the answer became doubly taboo.

For Dowd, like every other military pilot, the flying fraternity turned out to be the sort that had outer and inner chambers. No sooner did the novitiate demonstrate his capabilities in the outermost chamber and gain entrance to the next . . . than he discovered that he was once again a novitiate insofar as entry through the *next* door was concerned . . . and on and on the series goes. Moreover, in carrier training the tests confronted the candidate, the eternal novitiate, in more rapid succession than in any other form of flying.

He first had to learn to fly a propeller-driven airplane. Perhaps a quarter of an entering class might be eliminated, washed out, at this stage. Then came jet training and formation flight. As many as 50 percent of those left might wash out at these stages. But in naval flying, on top of everything else, there was the inevitable matter of . . . the heaving greasy skillet. That slab of metal was always waiting out in the middle of the ocean. The trainees first practiced touching down on the shape of a flight deck painted on an airfield. They'd touch down and then gun right off. This was safe enough—the shape didn't move, at least—but it could do terrible things to, let us say, the gyroscope of the soul. *That shape—it's so damned small!* And more novitiates washed out. Then came the day, without warning, when they were sent out over the ocean for the first of many days of reckoning with the skillet. The first day was always a clear day with little wind and a calm sea. The carrier was so steady it seemed to be resting on pilings—but what a bear that day was!

When Dowd was in training, aviators learned to land on the flight deck with the aid of a device that bore the horrible, appropriate name of the "meatball." This was a big mirror set up on the deck with a searchlight shining into it at a 3-degree angle— the angle of the flight deck—so that it reflected at the same angle. The aviator was to guide himself onto the deck by keeping the great burst of light, the meatball, visible in the center of the mirror. And many, many good souls washed out as they dropped like a brick toward the deck and tried to deal with that blazing meatball. Those who survived that test perhaps thought for a brief moment that at last they were regulars in Gideon's Army. But then came night landings. The sky was black, and the sea was black, and now that hellish meatball bobbed like a single sagging star in outer space. Many good men "bingoed" and washed out at this juncture. The novitiate was given three chances to land on the deck. If he didn't come in on his first or second approach and flew by instead, then he had to make it on his third, or the word "bingo!" would sound over his earphones—and over the entire flight deck, as he well knew—meaning that he would have to fly back to shore and land on a nice, safe immovable airfield . . . where everyone likewise knew he was a poor sad Bingo coming in from the carrier. It didn't take many bingos to add up to a washout.

One night, when Dowd had just started night training, the sea and the wind seemed to be higher, the clouds seemed lower, the night blacker than he thought possible. From up in the air the meatball seemed to bob and dart around in a crazy fashion, like a BB under glass in one of those roll-'em-in-the-hole games you hold in the palm of your hand. He made two passes and leveled off a good two hundred feet above the ship each time. On the third time around . . . it suddenly seemed of supreme, decisive, eternal importance that the word "bingo" not sound over *his* earphones. He fought the meatball all the way down in a succession of jerks, shudders, lurches, and whifferdills, then drove his plane onto the deck through sheer will, practically like a nail. The fourth and last deck wire caught him, and he kept the throttle pushed forward into the "full military power" position, figuring he was on the verge of boltering off the end and would have to regain altitude instanteously. He had his head down and his hand thrust forward, with his engine roaring—for how long?—God knows—before it dawned on him that he was actually down safe and could get out. The whole flight deck was waiting for him to shut off his damned engine. As he climbed down from the aircraft, he heard the skipper's voice boom out over the speaker system:

"How do you like flying now, Lieutenant?"

He noted with some satisfaction, however, that they then closed down the deck because of the weather. And was he *now* in the fraternity at last? . . . Hardly. He was just *beginning*. Everything he had learned to do so far became merely the routine. He was now expected to perform such incredible stunts day in and day out, under conditions of fleet operations and combat.

Being a carrier pilot was like being a paratrooper in that it took a while to learn how many different ways you could be killed in the course of an ordinary operation. A fellow F-4 jock, a friend, an experienced aviator, comes in one night low on fuel, not sure he has enough for a second pass, touches down long, bolters, tries to regain altitude, can't, careens off the far end of the deck, fifty thousand pounds of metal and tubes, and sinks without a trace. It all happens in a matter of seconds, *just like that.* Another friend, with even more experience, a combat veteran, *gets his* without moving a muscle. He's in his F-4, in the flight line, waiting for his turn on the catapult, when the ship up ahead somehow turns at the wrong angle, throttles up without a deflection shield behind it, and the whole fifteen tons of thrust hits his F-4, and the man and his guy-in-back and the ship are blown off the deck like a candy wrapper and are gone forever—in an instant, a snap of the fingers, *just like that.*

Yet once an aviator was in combat, all that, too, became simply the given, the hazards of everyday life on the job, a mere backdrop. From now on one found new doors, new tests, coming up with a mad rapidity. Your first day in combat . . . your first bombing run . . . first strafing run . . . the first time you're shot at . . . the first time you see a SAM . . . which also means the first time you dive for the deck straight into the maw of the flak cannons . . . the first time your ship gets dinged by flak . . . and the first time you *see someone else* in your own formation blown out of the sky over the North—and in many ways what an aviator saw with his own eyes was more terrible than the sudden unseen things happening to himself.

For Dowd and Garth Flint this came one day during a bombing run near the Iron Triangle. They were closing in on the target, barreling through the eternal cloud cover, unable to see even the ships in their own wing, when all at once a great livid ghost

came drifting straight across their path, from left to right. It was
an F-4. It had taken a direct hit, and smoke was pouring out of
the cockpit. The smoke enveloped the fuselage in the most
ghostly fashion. The pilot had cobbed it to starboard in a furious
effort to reach the water, the gulf, to try to bail out where Navy
rescue planes could reach them. In the blink of an eye the ghastly
cartridge disappeared, swallowed up by the clouds. They would
never make it. Dowd and Flint plowed on to the target, following their wing command, even though the gunners below obviously had dead range on the formation. To have done anything
else would have been unthinkable.

Unthinkable, to be sure. By late 1967 thinkable/unthinkable
played on a very narrow band. The options had been cut back
sharply. Both Navy and Air Force fliers were *getting theirs* at a
rate that was "astronomical and unacceptable," by ordinary logic,
as Jack Broughton had said. But fliers with a hundred missions
over the North were people who by now had pulled the rope ladder up into the pulpit. Somehow they had removed their ties
with the ordinary earth. They no longer lived on it. Home and
hearth, loved ones and dear ones—it wasn't that they had consciously lost their love or dear regard for such folks and such
things . . . it was just that the dear folks back home were . . . so
far away, back there through such an incalculable number of
chambers and doors. The fliers over the North now lived in, or
near, the fraternity's innermost room. Or, at the very least, they
now knew *who it was,* finally, who had access to that room. It was
not merely he who could be called "brave." No, it was he who
was able to put his hide on the line in combat and then had the
moxie, the reflexes, the experience, the coolness to pull it back in
the last yawning moment—and then was able to go out again *the
next day,* and the next day, and every next day, and do it all over
again, even if the series proved infinite. It was the *daily routine* of
risking one's hide while operating a hurtling piece of machinery
that separated military flying from all other forms of soldiering
and sailoring known to history.

Even *without going into combat* career Navy fighter pilots stood one chance in four of dying in an accident before their twenty years were up, and one chance in two of having to punch out, eject by parachute, at some point. In combat, especially in Vietnam, God knew what the figures were. The Pentagon was not saying. No, the Pentagon itself seemed bent on raising the ante to ridiculous heights, imposing restrictions that every aviator knew to be absurd. And "the nation"? "our country"? "the folks back home"? They seemed to have lost heart for the battle. But even that realization seemed . . . so far away, back through so many doors. Finally, there was only the business of the fraternity and the inner room.

All of the foregoing was out-of-bounds in conversation. Nevertheless, there it was. The closest aviators came to talking about it was when they used the term "professionalism." Many extraordinary things were done in the name of professionalism. And when everything else went wrong, this professionalism existed like an envelope, in the sense that each airplane was said to have a certain "performance envelope." Inside, inside that space, the aviators remained one another's relentless judges right up to the end, when not a hell of a lot of people outside seemed to care any longer. They were like casebook proof of something an English doctor, Lord Moran, had written forty years before. Moran had been a doctor treating soldiers in the trenches during the First World War, and he wrote one of the few analytical studies ever addressed specifically to the subject of bravery: *The Anatomy of Courage.* In the wars of the future, he said, aerial combat, not soldiering, would have "first call on adventurous youth." But the bravery of these adventurers, he said, would have a curiously detached quality. For the pilot, "love of the sport—success at the game—rather than sense of duty makes him go on."

The unspoken things! *Bye borty-bibe* . . . every morning when he woke up and rolled out of bed in his stateroom, the components of the game of high-low lit up in every aviator's brain, and he would all too literally calculate the state of his soul that morn-

ing by the composition of his bowel movement, with diarrhea being the worst sign of all. Well, not quite the worst; for occasionally one would hear some poor soul in another cubicle of the
head . . . vomiting. One would be curious . . . but in another way
one would just as soon not know who it was. (After all, he might
be in my wing.) Since none of this could be spoken, demeanor
was everything. (*Only your laundryman knows for sure!*) It *was* like
jousting! One *did* return to the carrier like a knight! . . . or as
near to knightly status as was likely to be possible in an age of
mimeographed flight assignments and mandatory debriefings.

The most beautiful possible moments came when you brought
your aircraft back to the deck from battle half shot up. Just a
few weeks ago Dowd and Garth Flint came back with an
85-millimeter shell hole shot clear through a rear stabilizer wing.
It looked as if you could put your arm through it, and it was no
more than a yard from the fuselage. Dowd and Flint had scarcely
opened the cockpit before the Mouseketeers, the deckhands,
were gaping at the damage. Dowd climbed down to the deck,
took off his helmet, and started walking away. Then, as if he'd
just remembered something, he turned about and said to the on-
lookers: "Check that stabilizer, will you? Think maybe we
caught a little flak."

How gloriously bored! The unspoken, unspeakable things!
All the gagged taboos!

No doubt that was what made American airmen, while on
leave, the most notorious bar patrons in the Philippines, Japan,
and Thailand during the Vietnam years. In keeping with a tradition as old as the First World War, drink and drunkenness
gave pilots their only license to *let it out*. Not to talk about the unspoken things—not to break the taboo—but to set free all the
strangled roars, screams, bawls, sighs, and raving yahoos. Emotion displayed while drunk didn't count. Everybody knew that.
One night Dowd was drinking at a bar at Cubi Point with an
A-4 pilot named Starbird. It was getting to that hour of the night
when you're so drunk you can't hear any more. Your skull itself

is roaring and your screams and songs get beaten back by the gale. The bartender announces that the bar is now closed. He slides a brass pole under the handles on the tops of the big beer coolers behind the bar and locks them shut. Starbird reaches across the bar and grabs the brass pole and emits a roar of sheer gorilla fury and pulls it up out of its mooring, until it's looped in the middle like a piece of spaghetti, and announces: "The bar just reopened."

After a long season of such affronts by many roaring souls, Navy bars and officers' clubs in Subic Bay began ruling themselves off limits to pilots returning from tours in the North (Yankee Station). Then came a gesture from on high that Dowd would never forget. Admiral Red Hyland himself sent out a directive, to all clubs and pubs within the purview of the Fleet, saying: It has come to my attention that the cocktail lounge conduct of aviators returning from Yankee Station has occasioned some negative responses. This is to inform all hands that the combat conduct of these men has been exemplary, despite the most trying conditions, and now hear this: THEY WILL BE ACCORDED THE FULL PRIVILEGES OF OFFICERS AND GENTLEMEN! (For you I bend the brass! The bars just reopened!)

At last!—someone had come close to saying it! to putting it into words! to giving a tiny corner of the world some actual inkling that they just might have . . . the ineffable . . . *it!*

That memo, like all memos, soon vanished down the memory hole. Yet it meant more to Dowd than any medal he ever got.

HIGH OR LOW? THE WEATHER DOESN'T GET ANY BETTER AS they pull closer to Haiphong, and Dowd decides to play it low. It looks like the kind of overcast the SAM's like best, high and solid. Dowd, with Brent off his wing, comes into Haiphong at about two hundred feet at close to Mach I. Suddenly they break out of the mist and they're over the harbor. They bank for one turn around it, which immediately cuts their speed down to about 450 knots. It's peaceful, just another inexplicable stroll in Haiphong Park. The overcast is down to four hundred feet, meaning it's hopeless so far as a bombing strike is concerned. Besides, the inevitable third-party ships are welded in . . .

The weather is so bad, it's as if the enemy has decided to take a holiday from the war, knowing no bombers will be coming in. There's no sense loitering, however, and Dowd heads out for a look at Cam Pha and Hon Gay, two ports north of Haiphong. High or low . . . Dowd stays down low. There's nothing below but a smattering of islands.

All at once Dowd sees a streak of orange shoot up over the nose on the port side. Garth Flint, in the back seat, sees another streak come up under the nose on the starboard . . . They both know at once: tracer bullets . . . *They go to school with the tracer bullets* . . . The tracers show the gunners whether or not they're near the mark . . . and without any doubt they're near the mark. Then they hear a sound like *twack* . . . It sounds like nothing more than a good-size rock hitting an automobile . . . the shot hit the bottom of the nose section . . . Dowd immediately cobs it, gives it full power in a furious bid to get up into the cloud cover and out over the gulf. Every warning light on the panel is lit up red, but he still has control of the plane. Smoke starts pouring into the cockpit. The heat is so intense he can barely touch sections of the panel. It's so hot he can hardly hold the controls. The fire seems to be in the hydraulics system of the wheel well. He tries to vent the cockpit, but the vent doesn't work. Then he blows the canopy off to try to clear the smoke, but the smoke pours out so heavily he still can't see. Everything metal is becoming fiercely hot. He wonders if the ejection mechanism will still work. He can hardly hold the stick.

For Garth Flint, in back, with the canopy gone, it's as if a hurricane has hit, a hurricane plus smoke. Maps are blowing all over the place, and smoke is pouring back. It's chaos. They're going about 350 knots, and the rush of air is so furious Flint can no longer hear anything on the radio, not even from Dowd. He wonders: Can we possibly get back onto the carrier if the smoke is this bad and Dowd can't hear radio communications? Oddly, all his worries center on this one problem. An explosion right in front of him! In the roiling smoke, where Dowd used to be, there's a metal pole sticking up in the air. It's made of sections, like a telescope. It's something Flint's never seen before ... the fully sprung underpinning of an F-4 ejection system, sticking up in the air as they hurtle over the Gulf of Tonkin. This spastic pole sticking up in the front seat is now his only companion in this stricken ship going 350 knots. Dowd has punched out!

Flint stares at the pole for perhaps two or three seconds, then pulls the ring under his seat. He's blasted out of the ship, with such force that he can't see.

Meanwhile, Dowd's furious ride is jerked to a halt by his parachute opening. He assumes Garth is floating down ahead of him. In fact, Dowd had yelled over the radio for Garth to eject and assumed he was on his way, not knowing Garth couldn't hear a word he said. Considering the way he had cobbed the engine and turned the plane to starboard and out over the gulf, Dowd expects to see water as he comes down through the clouds. Instead, little islands—and the live possibility of capture—are rising up toward him.

Reprieve! The wind carries him about a quarter mile from shore. Just the way the survival training told you, he prepares to shuck his parachute before he hits the water, at the same time keeping his life raft uninflated so the people onshore can't spot him so easily. He hits the water ... it's surprisingly cold ... he inflates the flotation device he's wearing—but feels himself being dragged under. The water, which looked so calm from above, is running five- to seven-foot swells. It pitches up and down in front of him and beneath him, and he's being dragged under. He can't comprehend it—the parachute, which he thought he had so skillfully abandoned at the textbook-proper second, has somehow wrapped around his right leg in the slosh of the swells and he's going under. He pulls out the knife that they're issued for just such a situation. But the nylon cords are wet and the damned knife won't cut them. He's going under. For the first time since the flak hit, the jaws of the Halusian Gulp have opened. *I'm going to die.* At first it's an incredible notion. Then it's infuriating. To die by drowning out in this squalid pond after a ten-cent shootdown on a weather-recce mission—it's humiliating! Another fly-boy disappears into the Cosmic Yawn! He's swept by a wave of the purest self-pity. It's actually about to happen—*his death*—the erasure of John Dowd from human existence—in a few seconds—*just like that!* The ineffable talent, the mystical power—*it!*—that let him hang his hide out over the Jaws and always pull it back—he *doesn't* have it, after all!—he is no more special than the hundreds of other pilots who have already been swallowed up over the North! It's pathetic. It's a miserable and colossal affront. His whole life does not roll before his eyes—only the miserable pity of the here and now. He does not think of home and hearth. He does not think of Mom at the shuttling sewing machine late at night or the poignancy of seeing one's own child daydreaming. No, there is only the here and now and the sum total of this total affront to all that comprises John Dowd—being dragged down in a fish pond by a parachute, holding in his hand a knife that the Navy issued for a task that it won't perform—it's utterly piteous and pathetic! . . . *Jesus! How I pity myself now!* . . . And that makes him furious. He gives the parachute a ferocious yank. Whuh?—in that very explosion of the final anger he discovers something: the damned thing is caught—not around his leg but on his knee-board! . . . The board is attached to his flight suit so he can jot down figures, keep charts handy, whatever . . . one last breath! Now he's completely underwater . . . He can't see . . . He grabs the knee-board and rips it off his flight suit . . . a miracle! . . . he's free! . . . The parachute is gone . . . the death anchor . . . He bobs back to the surface . . . Christ! . . . the hell with the colossal affront of fate . . . There's only *now!* . . . Never mind! . . . He inflates the raft, as it says in the manual . . . He's on the side of manual now! . . . Oh

yes! . . . Navy-issue! . . . Why not! . . . He climbs on the raft . . .
He's not drowning any more, he's on his belly on a raft swooping
up and down with the swells of the gulf . . . Never mind the
past! . . . He scans the water and the nearby island . . . Not miserable Fate, but islanders with guns . . . That's what he's looking
for . . . Is that one of them? . . . But on the water . . . there's
Garth! . . . Flint is on a raft about two hundred yards away, bob-
bing in and out of Dowd's line of vision . . . It's all shaping up . . .
Never mind Fate! The hell with colossal affronts! He's pulled it
back after all—out of the Jaws . . .

Meanwhile, Dick Brent, in the other F-4B, has seen Dowd and
Flint eject. After about fifteen minutes of diving and fishing
down through the clouds, Brent spots them on the water below
and radios the position. Brent sees a few people on the shore of an
island, looking out toward the two men, but the islands don't
seem to be making any attempt to go out by boat to retrieve
Garth and Dowd, which also means capture them. (In fact, the islanders had long since learned to leave well enough alone. American pilots in the water were often followed by screaming rescue
aircraft that blew every boat out of the tub.)

After about another thirty minutes Spads are coming in low
over the water. To Garth Flint it appears as if the Spad pilots
don't see him, only Dowd. Over his emergency radio Flint says:
"If you see two pilots, rock your wings." One of the Spads rocks
its wings. The Spads call in a helicopter known as a Big Mother.
The helicopter, too, heads straight for Dowd. A morose thought
crosses Flint's mind: "He's a lieutenant, I'm only a lieutenant
(j.g.)—so they're picking him up first."

Then it dawns on him that they're going after Dowd because
he's in closer to shore and therefore more vulnerable to gunfire or
capture. Hell, it's going to be okay.

BACK ON THE *CORAL SEA* DOWD AND FLINT WERE DEBRIEFED IN
the ready room. They drank coffee and tried to warm up. The

china had a certain dignity. It was white with bands of blue about the rims and blue crests here and there. The silverware—now, that was rather nice. It was ornamental and heavy. The questions, came, one after the other, and they went through everything that happened. Yet during this debriefing the two men were waiting for *something else*. Surely, they would mention *something else*. But they didn't. It was a debriefing much like *every* debriefing. Just the facts! No quarter given! No slack in the line! Then the commander of their squadron said, with a note of accusation: "Why were you flying so low?"

Now, that was really too much! Why . . . you *bastard!* But they said nothing except the usual. What they wanted to say . . . well, how could they have put it into words? How, within the inner room, does one say: "My God, man, we've just been into the Jaws!—about as far into the goddamned Jaws as you can go and still come back again!—and you want to know why we flew so low! We've just been *there!* at the lost end of the equation! where it drops off the end of the known world! Ask us about . . . *the last things,* you bastard, and we will enlighten you!" There were no words in the chivalric code for such thoughts, however.

But all at once the skipper of the *Coral Sea,* the maximum leader, a former combat pilot himself, appeared—and he smiled! And that smile was like an emission of radio waves.

"We're glad to have you back, men."

That was all he said. But he smiled again! Such ethereal waves! Invisible but comprehensible, they said, "I know. I've been there myself." Just that!—not a sound!—and yet a doxology for all the unspoken things. How full my heart, O Lord!

Flint took one day off before going out on his next mission, on New Year's Eve. Dowd had suffered a back injury in the ejection from the F-4B, and so it was another two days before he climbed back into the metal slingshot, got slung off the skillet, and went flying over North Vietnam again.

chapter IV

The Commercial

A Short Story

THE BIBLE SAYS, "WOE BE TO THE CROWN OF PRIDE, FOR IT shall be trodden under feet," and if that be true, I was due to get stomped from the moment I said I'd do it. I built it up so big in my mind. That commercial was going to take care of so many things. I built it up to where it was going to change my life! I'm not talking about the money I got for it, which was $5,000, because I mean I *make* $65,000 a year from the Astros. It was some other things. That commercial was going to eliminate some of the things I had to live behind, all this stuff they say . . . like, "Willie Hammer can hit a baseball but he doesn't have . . . *this* . . . or he doesn't have *that* . . ." Hey, it's going to be embarrassing to get into this stuff, man! It has to do with pride, and like it says, "Woe be to the crown of pride"!

What I am saying is, yes, I got whipped, but I got whipped in a way that had nothing to do with cracking my head. That was an accident purely. I slipped and fell and hit my head, and that is all. They say I was "knocked out." I'd say I was more like stunned.

What burns me up is that some people think Foley did it. How can they believe that? Take a look at that sucker! He's an *ad*vertising man! He's nothing but a pillow-butt Irishman. I can't stand to see a man who doesn't keep himself in any better condition than that. It's hard to tell white people's age, but he isn't very old. He must be thirty-five, along in there. He's got these little small white hands—and then check out the rest of him. The rest of him is a fat factory! He's chugging away and putting out the fat!

I'll tell you when he got his licks in. That was while they were shooting the commercial. He had me whipped there, and that I will admit; him and his whole bunch of Ritz crackers. That's what I call your modern up-to-date cracker, your cracker who is too liberal and too well educated and has his necktie pulled up too tight to trifle with techniques like yelling *jigaboo* or *burr-head* from out of the right-field stands.

The night before I was supposed to do the commercial they picked me up at the New York Hilton, Foley and his sidekick, a little snapper called Norm Lane. We were supposed to get acquainted and so on. This Norm Lane was a bouncy little number who chuckled and nodded at anything anybody said. They took me over to a place called the Palm Restaurant on Second Avenue. All the way over they kept raving about the Palm Restaurant. They kept saying, "Fabulous steaks." Foley would say it and then Norm Lane would nod a lot and say the same thing. They said it about twelve times.

We get there, and to be frank about it, the Palm Restaurant reminds me of one of those Creole restaurants in Houston where the gumbo soup has grains of sand in it and they let somebody's nephew paint murals up on the wall. The Palm Restaurant had a lot of really bush-league drawings up on the wall, mostly of celebrities nobody ever heard of.

But it was popular, all right. There must be a lot of people in New York as crazy about the Palm Restaurant as Foley and Norm Lane. It was packed with well-dressed white people, all of them grinning and babbling until it looked like their teeth were boiling. I was the only colored person in there, but I didn't mind that. Sometimes I enjoy that. If you're a professional athlete in top condition and you walk into a place full of ordinary men, it's like you're built in neon. And any athlete who tells you he doesn't know that feeling is telling a lie. It's in the way you carry yourself. It's in your neck and the set of your jaw. Your power always shows through. If you have a neck size 17 and you pull your shoulders down a little, it makes your neck fan out like a cobra. And if you're dark like I am and you always wear a white shirt like I do—then they really turn around and check you out! I hadn't reached the point where I could walk into a restaurant in New York and people would say, "There's Willie Hammer," but I can read it on their faces when white men are looking around and saying to themselves, "That black dude there has something about him. I wonder who he is."

Foley and Norm Lane were right in their element in the Palm Restaurant. They were knocking back drinks and talking a frozen rope. Some old white snooker comes in with one of those girls you see with the chalky-white skin and dark-red lipstick and slumped-over shoulders and a nylon blouse that her tits show through and the kind of shoes that girls like, the platforms, with the five-inch sole and the seven-inch heels, silver-colored. She comes wobbling in on top of the shoes, and everybody does a number on her. Foley says he loves this Second Avenue because it's "the nipple tango" from one end to the other. He has a lot of expressions like "the nipple tango." He'll call somebody "Mr. Transistors" and after a while you'll figure out that what he means is, the man is cold-blooded, he has no heart. Or he'll say "slip into the linen envelope" and he just means "go to bed." Every time Foley or Norm Lane get off one of their lines, they're looking at me, as if I'm very tight into the conversation the whole time, only they're really just batting it back and forth with each other.

"I don't know what it's like in Houston, Willie," Foley says, "but it's a laugh and a half here. We can't hire a secretary in our office any more. She has to be an 'administrative assistant.' I'm not kidding you. And so then what do they do?"

Norm Lane is nodding and grinning like he couldn't agree more, but what he says is: "Foley doesn't understand Jewish girls, Willie."

Foley steps right over that one, he just keeps his number going: "They don't want to be treated like sex objects, right? So they wear pants to the office, but these pants are so unbelievably snug in the rug—"

"Foley doesn't understand—"

"—and they don't wear bras, and the whole office is like one big nipple tango. What I'd like to know is, what would they do if they *wanted* to be sex objects!"

"Foley doesn't understand Jewish girls, Willie," says Norm Lane.

Foley says, "What do Jewish girls have to do with it?"

Norm Lane says, "Are you kidding? Look around some time. Without Jewish girls there wouldn't *be* any women's liberation. The peep show is just to give you a little tingle, a little uppie, prior to surgery."

"For chrissake, Norm. Don't pay any attention to him, Willie," says Foley. "He's out to lunch."

Foley sounds a little ticked off, although I don't know why, because the only Jewish person at the table is Norm Lane himself. But anyway, Foley turns his back on him. He turns to a waiter and tells him to bring another bottle of wine. So Norm Lane says to the waiter: "Yeah, and bring him a new conversation while you're at it."

This Norm Lane was Foley's yes-man but, like you see, he'd agree with him and then put an edge on it or a twist to it or just try to top him.

THE MORE FOLEY AND NORM LANE WENT ON, THE MORE UN-comfortable I got. You could tell that the reason they made out I was in the conversation was that I wasn't even close to being in it. It's a funny thing being a professional athlete and being well known. When you're with people you never met before, for about the first fifteen minutes they're impressed that you're even there, that you're actually breathing the same air they're breathing. It's like you have a glow and they're tickled pink about the light. But after a while you see them looking at you. They've got their heads cocked. Then it dawns on you. They're waiting for you to *say* something! And not just anything, something *outta sight!* They're waiting for you to be a *character.* They're waiting for a little hot-shot *personality* to go with the hot-shot athlete they see on the ball field. If you happen to be somebody who believes in self-control and you don't believe in saying something if you don't have anything worth saying—well, the hell with you! I can't tell you how many times I've met people and afterward I know they've gone away saying, "Well, he's nothing but a piece of furniture!" That goes double with the sportswriters. I get so tired. If the sportswriters come around and you don't have a line of cool breeze and a little smoke to blow up their fannies, they start writing that you're "soft-spoken," "unassuming," "reserved," "remote," "aloof," you're "a man of quiet dignity," you "let the bat do the talking"—and what this really is, it's a code. What they're really saying is, "Hey, chief! This guy's dull! a deadhead! a washout! poor copy! nerve gas! He'll put you to sleep!"

So I keep trying to think up something to get into the conversation with Foley and Norm Lane. I want to show these two New York advertising aces some live wire. I'm racking my brain. Do you know that feeling when you're at a table and you're being left out of the conversation and you're waiting for something to come up, any subject you have a little nugget of information about, anything you can throw into the conversation—just so they won't think you're a deadhead? Well, just then Foley starts talking about all the pushovers Joe Frazier fought after he beat Ali, such as Terry Daniels. *Terry Daniels?* Hey, I *know* Terry Daniels! I know the man *personally!* Hey! Wait! I got a *nugget* here!—but Norm Lane is in there like a flash and he's wondering if boxing will survive as a big-time sport after Ali retires, and Foley says, hell, television can keep any sport alive, he saw his nine-year-old son watch a whole *curling* match on the *Wide World of Sports,* which reminds Norm Lane of a vacation he took in Scotland and it was the worst vacation he ever took, which reminds Foley that the only place worse than Scotland is Finland, because trying to find something to do in Helsinki is like trying to sell encyclopedias at a funeral—and I'm still sitting there saying to myself—"Terry Daniels! Is it too late for me to get in there with Terry Daniels!" Too late? Why, those suckers were already halfway around the world and heading for Asia and I hadn't even gotten my mouth open.

So I just sat there in the Palm Restaurant and let the noise and the gabble roll over me. But to be truthful, there was more than those two jivemongers that was bothering me. I had one of those time bombs that you get. It was sitting in the back of my head at all times, like the tooth that's got to be pulled sooner or later. This time bomb was about the script for the commercial that I'd be doing the next day. I'd had the script for a month, and the first time I read it I knew I had a problem. But I was afraid if I squawked about it, if I even raised a peep about it, they might cancel the whole deal. That gives you an idea of how bad I wanted to do the commercial. I couldn't stand the thought of losing that beautiful shot, no matter what. I figured I could straighten out the script in the meantime. I figured I could think of something. So I kept putting it off. I didn't even want to talk to my lawyer about it. I didn't want to talk to my wife about it. I *especially* did not want to talk to my wife about it. I could see Loretta backing me up against the wall with a prime-time Loretta lecture, with a smoking hot mess of words that not even blue darters like your Foleys and Norm Lanes could keep up with. I didn't want to talk to anybody about it. I didn't want to have to think about it. I would take care of it when I had an opening. In other words, I had my head stuck about three feet down in the sand.

So here I am in the Palm Restaurant the night before they're supposed to shoot the commercial, and I still don't bring it up. "Well," I'm saying to myself, "these guys are half in the bag now. They're knocking back the wine and talking a coastal fog. Yeah, there's no point to bringing up this heavy business right now . . . There'll be some way to do it tomorrow . . ." You know how that number goes.

THEY TOLD ME TO BE AT A STUDIO OVER ON EAST FORTY-eighth Street, X.T.O. Teletronics, at eight-thirty in the morning. At eight-thirty sharp I came in there carrying a duffel bag with six Louisville Slugger baseball bats in it and two dozen official National League baseballs. I felt a little funny about that, coming in there carrying a duffel bag. I mean, here I got on a $400 gabardine suit, tailor-made, a $32 shirt, a $15 Italian silk necktie, and a brand-new pair of McAfee shoes from Saks Fifth Avenue that set me back $87.50, and I come in toting a duffel bag full of bats and balls. But I was determined to be handing out those bats and balls. You're going to laugh when I tell you why. Woe be to the crown of pride!

The studio was nothing like I figured on, because all I had to go by was television studios. This place was huge. It was big as an airplane hangar in there, only gloomier and full of all kinds of scaffolds and equipment and lines running everywhere. The ceiling was up so high, maybe five or six stories high, it was just a big black gloom up there, and they didn't even try to hang lights from it. All the lights were on poles and stands sticking up in the air, spotlights and floodlights and lights with flaps and reflectors. It was hard to get your bearings or make out anything in depth, because one second you're in the gloom and then *bam!* a big shot of light hits you in the face.

Finally I make out Foley and Norm Lane and the rest of them from the advertising agency, but there seem to be thirty or forty other people besides, people fooling around with microphones and lights and even a forklift—and this kind of threw me, too. I thought it was going to be half a dozen people and a camera. Everybody was white except for one kid who runs errands and plays the fool. This kid, when somebody would tell him to go do something, he'd point at the man and say, "I gotcha covered!" and roll his eyes and then go do it.

Foley and Norm Lane come on over and make a big fuss over me and start introducing me around. I hoisted the duffel bag and unveiled the bats and balls. I think they really liked getting those things. I was passing them out and I'd say, "I thought maybe you all might like to give these to your kids."

There was a little backing and filling over who was going to get the bats, because there were only six of them. They had my signature on them, "Willie Hammer." Foley made sure this one older ace got one right away. He was from the company that made the perfume we were going to do the commercial about, Fabrilex. He had one of those big thin noses that some white people have. He thanked me for the bat and took a grip on it like he was at the plate, and he smiled. When he smiled, his mouth had a way of creeping up under his big nose. Foley points to him and says, "Now, *that* would scare the *hell* out of a pitcher, wouldn't it, Willie?"

Foley was ribbing this man, but at the same time he was doing a little friendly fanny-rubbing. He was showing this man a lot of attention. Foley acted toward this man the way Norm Lane acted toward Foley. Foley was the big organizer and the big noise around here, but the man from the Fabrilex Company was the main man in this setup.

The man said to me, "This is a *heavy bat*," and, to be honest, I was grateful for that remark, because it gave me a chance to do some talking and not just stand there like a fence post. I told the man how I like a 36-ounce bat with a big handle because it has better balance and I can control the heavy end better. I have a whole theory about controlling the heavy end of the bat. I have a whole *speech* about controlling the heavy end of the bat. It is the only speech I do have, and I was grateful for the chance to do my number. A lot of the studio crew were gathered around, and they were all quieted down, listening, looking very serious, as if to say, "Hey, this man is hitting .380 in the National League and we best to pay attention." I liked that; it made me feel like I had a grip on the situation.

With everybody standing there, my friend with the nose let me know he'd played a little ball himself, in college some place. He just slipped it in, but he made *sure* he slipped it in, if you know what I mean, and I liked that, too. It's a thing I've noticed everywhere, and this man, this executive of a big corporation like Fabrilex, he was no different from anybody else. This country is full of about 100 million men who played a little ball, some sport, some time, some place. And wherever it was, it was there they left whatever feeling of manhood they ever had. It grew there and it bloomed there and it died there, and now they work at some job where the manhood thing doesn't matter, and the years roll by. But they've got this little jar of ashes they carry around . . . "I once played a little ball . . ." They see a professional athlete, and it stirs up the memories . . . They can feel the breeze.

BUT WAIT A MINUTE, WE GOT TO—WITHOUT ANY TO-DO THEY TAKE me out in the middle of the studio and set me down in a little swivel chair. It's like the lights are all right down on top of your head, and hovering above you, in the gloom out beyond, you can make out the shadows of the monster rigs of equipment and the stagehands closing in.

I told myself, "Big boy, you've let it get down to the nub, haven't you? How you going to take care of that script in front of an army!"

The director takes a seat in a little chair facing mine. He is the weirdest-looking sucker in the room. He was one of those white guys you see now who is pushing fifty but he wants to look like a kid. He's got on tennis shoes and a blue-jean outfit, the jacket and the pants, and he's nearly bald on top, but he's let the hair around the sides grow real long, and it looks like it must've been kinky but he conked it, and it hangs down to his shoulders like a hula skirt around his bald head. The man's a sketch. The whole time he's smiling at me most warmly, like we have a most deep understanding, us two.

"All right, Willie," he says, "I'm just going to run through it once, the way you'll be doing it."

He has the script in one hand and a bottle of the perfume I'm supposed to be endorsing in the other and the smile on his face and the conked hair on his head fluffed out in all its glory.

"The camera will be on you, Willie. You'll be looking right into it. When you start talking, the idea is to sound as if you're just *finishing* a commercial. You're just winding it up. You're saying: 'And so, men . . .' "

And here the man starts putting a lot of acting into it. He throws it into his shoulders and twists his body, which makes all that shrubbery on his head flop around.

He says, " 'And so, men, if you want a cologne that's a *real man's* cologne . . . smooth, cool, and *very* romantically inclined . . . take it from me, Willie Hammer. Do what I've done. Switch to the new . . .'

"And then you hesitate, Willie. You pull your head back, like this. You look at the bottle of cologne in your hand as if you didn't even know it was there, as if it's some kind of *strange object* you've got there. How did *this* get here?

"You're staring at the bottle. And then you say, real slow, as if you're reading the name on the bottle for the first time and you can't make it out—you say, '. . . the new . . . Charlie Magnet?' You say it like a question, as if you're saying, 'What the hell is this thing and what have they written on it?' You say, 'Charlie Magnet?' Like that.

"And then, Willie, you look off-camera, as if there's somebody off here to the side who you're looking at. You look off like this, and you say: 'Hey! What is this Charlie Magnet jazz!'

"Got it? You're still holding the bottle up like this, Willie, and now the camera leaves your face and comes up tight on your hand and the bottle and the label, and the viewer will see the actual name of the cologne for the first time: Charlemagne."

Only he says it softly, the way somebody might say, "Reverend Jones."

"And then, Willie, the announcer comes in with the voice-over. He says, 'This Charlie Magnet, Willie Hammer, is Charlemagne, the new King of Colognes for the man who likes it on top . . . especially created by Fabrilex to bring out the king in you.'

"At that point the bottle montages into an outline in color and there's an animated sequence. It's really a fabulous animation, too, Willie, and I want you to see it, but we don't have to worry about that now.

"Anyway, the announcer, in the voice-over, will be saying: 'Before Charlemagne, a man's cologne was just a fragrance. Charlemagne is more. Charlemagne contains a totally new ancillodermal skin conditioner that brings out the full-bodied glow of the real man . . . *plus!* an exciting new fragrance created especially for Charlemagne by the famous Adam Chigneau . . . a fragrance that says *King* . . . after dark and in the dawn . . . Be a real magnet, Charlie . . . Score day and night . . . like Willie Hammer!'

"Then it cuts back to you, Willie. Now the camera is back on you, and you're looking at the bottle again, like you were before we cut away. You still look puzzled, but you're also smiling a little. You look quizzical."

And here the man gives me a demonstration of *quizzical*. He wraps his eyebrows around his nose and screws up his mouth and hooks his chin down over his collarbone.

"And then, Willie, you say: 'This Charlie Magnet here has all THAT?'"

"And the announcer's voice says: 'That's right, Willie.'"

"And then you look directly into the camera, and you open

your eyes wide, like this, in mock surprise, and you say: 'You know . . . I think I'll TRY it!'

"Then you drop the act, and you break into a big laugh, and the camera pulls back, and the word Charlemagne is super-imposed on the screen, and underneath it, in smaller letters, it says, 'The King. You're on top.' And in the background you're holding up the bottle and laughing. The viewer can see you com-pletely now, sitting in the chair and laughing and having a good time.

"It's a hell of a cute bit, I think, Willie. You say, 'You know . . . I think I'll TRY it!!!' "

And with this, the man does the laugh, too, only I never heard such a laugh in my life. It's like a scream. It's like he stuck his hand down his throat and brought a laugh up from out of his belly and he's holding it up over his head, bleeding.

Doesn't faze him at all, though. The next instant he's just look-ing at me with that Nurse Mary grin of his, and he's saying:

"Well . . . that's it. Shall we get to work?"

And that's about when she hit the fan.

Big boy! Your time just ran out!

Right here I had a feeling like all the air was rushing out of the place, creating a mighty vacuum . . . a mighty emptiness like outer space . . . and into that vast and mighty silence here comes a single sound . . . a voice! . . . the voice of some countrified nig-ger, saying:

"Naw."

It was me, of course! It was me, sending this brilliant message out into the vastness, up toward the monster rigs and the multi-tudes of X.T.O. Teletronics, New York City, Network TV, U.S.A. . . . *naw* . . . and that word was swelling up inside of that monster place like a big brown oil bubble, and I could see the whole bunch of them pulling away from the dumb trifling *messi-ness* of that one word I had cut loose!

And even in that very moment I couldn't understand how so much could be racing through my head and how so little could be coming out! I meant to be saying, "Hey, man, let's change a few words here and there! Hey—it'll only take a second!" But I was nearly paralyzed, because even here at the zero hour there were still two hard grabbers working on me, one of them screaming like Loretta and saying, "You can't do this!" and the other one, the golden mule, saying: "You got to! This is what you been waiting for all this time!" So the only sound that got out was "Naw."

But you can't leave it at that, sucker!

My brain labored powerfully, and I expanded upon the concept.

I said, "Naw. It sounds dumb."

"Whattayamean, Willie?" That is the director.

"Hey, what's up, Willie?" That was Foley, coming in from the edge of the set, out of the gloom.

"What's the matter with the man? What's he talking about?" That's my pal from Fabrilex, the ace with the nose, who played a little ball, talking to Foley.

The director waves Foley off, as if to say, "Let me handle this." Out loud he says, "Let's take a break."

Then he takes me over to the side, out of the lights, into the gloom by the rigs, and he starts talking to me in a low voice as if there's just the two of us and we're going to see what the trouble is. But I can feel Foley, the Fabrilex man, the monster rig, and all the giants of the gloom giving me a look you could pave a street with. The director is saying why don't I tell him exactly what the problem is. Why don't we talk it over. I've seen the script before, haven't I? I've had it for a month, haven't I? . . . Yeah . . . It didn't look so bad before now, did it? . . . Naw . . . Then why was it "dumb" now?

So I tried to tell him. I tried to get my thoughts together, but I couldn't think in that place. I was trying to think of some way to tell him without having to go into the *whole thing.*

I told him, "I don't like it where I'm supposed to say 'Charlie

Magnet.' That's what sounds dumb. How can I get out there and act like I can't read 'Charlemagne'?"

"Willie!" he says. "It's a gag! It's a cute bit. Naturally you know how to read the word. That's obvious. That's the whole point. You're so confident, you can make *fun* of yourself. The commercial makes fun of *it*self. It's actually a very sophisticated commercial. You should get involved in a *bad* commercial! I have! I know!"

The whole time he's talking I can also hear everything else in the room just as loud, people talking, things moving around, my buddy from Fabrilex saying, "He's *your* inspiration, Foley." The director keeps looking down at the floor and pulling his chin and disappearing inside his conked hair.

Finally I say, "Look, man. Why don't we just rewrite it a little . . . you know? . . . take the Charlie Magnet out. That's all I want."

He looks up at me for a second—and lifts his eyebrows and gives his mouth that little end-of-the-line smile, the one that says, "Willie, my dear friend, why don't you ask me to tell the rain to turn around and fall *up?*"

All of a sudden he pulls real close to me and puts his arm around my shoulders and he says: "Willie . . . goddamn it, I know exactly what you're thinking. But you can't take it that seriously, because nobody else will, including the people who watch it. You've got to tell yourself: 'It's *only a commercial.*' This isn't *my* life, either. I'm a *film*maker. I don't throw my heart and soul into a commercial. I come out here and do a professional job. I do a damned professional job. There's no one who does a *more* professional job. They get their money's worth—but that's all they're getting! And that's all they're getting from you! You're not putting your heart and soul on parade, either! We're both doing the thing. We're both using this thing as a vehicle. Trotsky used to—there's an old saying, 'You don't have to believe in the trolley company to get where you want to go.' Listen, I'm not going to let you look bad in this thing. That I promise you! Hell, you'll look great! So, for God's sake, don't you make *me* look bad. Let's just work together, baby, and get this thing over with and *forget* it."

"Baby," he says—and gives my shoulder a little squeeze! Brother! You 'n' me! These people are too much! They put on their blue jeans and their tennis shoes and they call you baby! Check it out, Mr. Soul Mate Funk! You're nuzzling up against a $400 suit and a pair of $87.50 McAfees!

MAN, WHAT DO I NEED SOME TURKEY LIKE YOU WITH HIS arms around me for ... when right this minute I can hear my wife's little lecture in my head: "Willie! It's not enough to hit baseballs and go down to Lashford's and have your pretty clothes made! You have a *responsibility!*" The responsibility of which she speaks is my responsibility to the Black People and to the Black Youth. Loretta's right; I could do a lot more than I've done, and I feel bad about that. She thinks the good light 'n' bright folks of Bayou Grove are looking at her as the wife of ... a Tom! Right!—even though I am the one who is *black,* and I am the one who grew up *on the street,* and she and the whole Bayou Grove crowd are the light 'n' brights who went to the university and never even had a bottle of soda pop with an *uneducated* young rascal before they met me—but none of that has anything to do these days with being Black Enough! When we give a party, you'll see a couple of lawyers looking light, bright, rich, and *ready* out by the wall of Aucuba bushes that cost me fifteen hundred dollars to put around the swimming pool, and they'll be saying:

"Well, don' none-a my clients care!"

"They better! Don' nobody hide the cob on a Jasper Charlie like that with a writ of mandamus or quashing a subpoena."

"I can dig it."

"Gon' take more'n the A.C.L.U., baby!"

"Uh-hunh. Don' say I said it, but a little bird tol' me De Judge gon' murphy that sucker with a certoriari an' he's gon' smack the dead an' that's gonna ice his you-know-what!"

Hide the cob? Smack the dead? I don't even know what these people are saying half the time. The only place I ever heard "smack the dead" before was in a card game they used to play out on the stoops called "coon can," and I know these light 'n' brights never got within ten miles of a game of coon can. Man, there's so much Soul amongst the rich, the smooth, and the creamy in Bayou Grove these days, James Brown would have to fall down on his knees and beg for driver training . . . And all the while I can see Loretta watching . . . Her retarded husband *looks* okay . . . It's just when the poor gugger tries to open his mouth that the situation gets embarrassing . . . That's the word! . . . They're all staring at *me* . . . wondering when I'm gon' Come Back . . . and get Black Enough!

All I need now is to do this Charlie Magnet trick on nation-wide TV . . . Can't you hear the rest already? . . . "Willie! You had to do it! You had to go steppin' 'n' fetchin' on nationwide TV, so everybody in town would know I was married to Super Tom!"

Man, I should walk out of here right now and tell you people to stuff your commercial in a very old place. And I would make that noble move, too . . . except for one little thing . . . I want to make a commercial so bad I can taste the icing!

You people don't even know what the nationwide TV com-mercial means to the big-league ballplayer, and you're the people who make them . . . There's so few players chosen that a lot of fellows in the big league, they de*fine* the superstar as the man who gets picked for the commercial. They begin to look at that man in a different way . . . "Hmmmmm . . . we got a famous cat on our hands . . . !" The colored players get chosen least of all, and they do complain. A bunch of players will be sitting around in the clubhouse watching TV, and somebody like Johnny Bench will come on doing his deodorant commercial, and you'll hear some colored player say:

"Shit . . . *Johnny Bench* . . . Hey, man, get busy and start a write-in campaign to those suckers. I sweat just as much as Johnny Bench and I got *more* home runs."

And some white player will say: "Yeah, you'd think they'd at least pick you guys for the toothpaste commercials."

"Why's that?"

"Hell, man, the only thing we like about you people is your perfect thirty-two!"

And the whole bunch of them, black and white, they'll laugh at stuff like that, because that shows they're cool, they're the Modern Ballplayer, they're above the color thing. But I stay out of this Race Razz. I see it as thin ice. I see a cool stick of shitfire with a wick on it. I say the only thing puts you above the color thing is getting the commercial itself. That says: "This man is so hot, he's such a giant, such a superstar, even white people buy what he endorses." This shuck word "superstar" is stuck in every brain! I have to take orders from the manager, while the superstar walks all over the manager and me, too. I have to double up in the hotels, while the superstar gets the single room or the suite. I go out and hit .334 lifetime, three full seasons, and I get sixty-five thousand a year, while the superstar like Reggie Jackson hits so low they don't even *mention* it in those big stories where they call him the "superduperstar" and put him on the cover of *Sports Illustrated. Two-sixty-four* lifetime, that supershuck is *seventy points* below me, and he gets more than a hundred thousand—but he's what the white sportswriters like. He's the Black Hot Dog. If your success happens to come from the same thing as the better class of white man's—namely, *self-control*—it's so long, Willie, and don't let the doorknob hit you in the butt on the way out.

That's why getting picked for this commercial is something unbelievable, like something wonderful that fell out of the sky. But you have to throw in this Charlie Magnet shit, don't you? You have to tell me to go out there and play Rastus in the Pineywoods . . . Anyway, man, maybe if I knew how to tell you all that, you'd see why it gives me no thrill to speak of when you hug me in your blue-jean arms and you call me baby and you tell me you understand.

THEY MUST HAVE SEEN THE SUCKER WASN'T GETTING ANY-where with me, because then the heavyweights started moving in. The next thing I know, Foley and Norm Lane are standing next to me, and the Fabrilex ace is just a few feet behind. Right away I know this is a new Foley I got to deal with. The fat little sucker isn't smiling like a perch any more! He and Norm Lane have on the matching long faces.

Foley says, "Okay, how we doing over here?"

The director says, "I don't know . . . I think it'll be all right."

Foley says, "How about it, Willie?"

I say, "Man . . . how can you expect somebody to go out there and act like they *can't read?*"

Foley says, "Willie"—but I can't believe what I'm hearing. He just lays out my name, out flat. Willie. He's got that tone that says, "Sonny boy, we've been giving you a lot of room to make your mess in, on account of your age, but as of right now . . . you're gonna commence to *act right!*" I can feel the man is about to jerk me around in front of all these people, but for some reason I've got no heart. I can't get my spirit up against the man, the way I did with this director here, and his whole number was that he was my *friend!*

"Willie"—he says my name again, and this time he turns his palms up and spreads out his arms as if to say, "You see all this, Willie, this huge place, these lights, these tremendous rigs, this studio, this advertising business, this network TV, this New York City, and above all . . . *us* . . . us terrific people, with the power and the talent—do you see all of *us* waiting for Willie Hammer to stop acting like a baby!"

"Willie," he says, for the third time, "you say you don't know how I expect anybody to do this commercial. For God's sake, man! Eleven *fam*ous men, in addition to yourself, eleven *profes-*

*sion*al *ath*letes, are doing this commercial, and they're doing it the *same* way you are. Nolan Perry has already *done* his. Brook Howard has done *his*. Tommy Cash has done *his*. Nobody, not one of them, has thought for *one second* that this commercial makes them look bad. They're not *idiots,* Willie! They all have agents, or a lawyer, like you do, and these guys don't live in a tree, either. Now, if it doesn't make them look bad, can you tell me why it'll make you look bad?"

The man was giving me a goddamn lecture! I couldn't believe it! I wanted to let him have it. I wanted to say, "You left out just one thing, fat boy. All those guys you mentioned are *white!*" But shit, all I said was: "I don't know about those guys. All I know is—why can't I do it the regular way?"

Foley says, "The regular way," and looks off in the distance.

I say. "The way—aw hell, man, you know what I'm talking about, the way Hank Aaron does it, what he says in the Brut commercial. He says, 'I use it. I like it.' He says, 'You use it. You'll like it.' The regular way, man! What's wrong with that?"

Foley says, "The Brut commercial!" and Norm Lane starts pursing his lips and shaking his head, in a way that says, "Poor Willie. And to think he used to have a full deck."

"Yeah!" I said. "The Brut commercial."

Foley says, "Willie, that kind of commercial—that's what *does* make you look bad. Not only bad—*dumb!* That's the old style. You can't *do* that any more. That commercial didn't do a thing for Hank Aaron."

"Willie, I'm glad you—" That was Norm Lane trying to break in.

"People aren't blind," Foley says. "They know athletes get paid money to stand up in front of a camera and say 'I use this' or 'I use that.' "

"Willie, I'm glad— Foley, let me say something—"

"This commercial doesn't do that," Foley says. "It does just the opposite. You're not being one of those jerks who gets up and says, 'Uhm Wullie Hummer un' uh use Chullymun.' You're saying, 'Hell, no, *I don't* use Charlemagne. I never even *heard* of it before! But it sounds good, and maybe I'll try it.' "

"Foley, let me say something," says Norm Lane. "Willie, I'm glad you mentioned Hank Aaron, because you want to know what really made Aaron look *terrific?* It wasn't the Brut commercial. It was the *Gillette commercial.*"

"That's right!" says Foley. "He's absolutely right, Willie!"

Norm Lane says, "You remember that series, don't you, Willie? They had Hank Aaron and Tom Seaver and Larry Csonka, and the voice-over says, *'I, Larry Csonka . . .'*

" 'I, Larry Csonka.'

" *'Do solemnly swear . . .'*

" 'Do solemnly swear.'

" *'To always use faithfully . . .'*

" 'To always use faithfully.'

" *'The new Gillette Platinum-Plus . . .'*

"And here the Csonka, or whoever, would start goofing it up. He'd say, 'The new Gillette plutonium platter.' "

Foley says, "They'd say, 'Gelatinous pitcher-a pus!' "

Norm Lane says, " 'A skillet of blistering schmutz!' "

Foley says, " 'A pillager village of lust!' "

They're going on this way . . . They're going crazy over this dumb Gillette commercial . . . They're laughing! singing! bawling with joy! . . . It's a duet . . . a concert . . .

I said, "Hank Aaron . . . did that commercial?"

Foley says, "Oh, God, yes."

Norm Lane says, "Oh, Christ, yes, yes. He was beautiful."

Foley says, "Not only that, Willie—and I'm not exaggerating—that commercial *made Hank Aaron!*"

Norm Lane says, "No question about it. It *defrosted* him!"

Foley says, "How many years did Aaron play before anybody really noticed him? How many home runs did he hit before anybody said, 'Hey, this guy is more than just a pretty fair country ballplayer'? About six hundred. And you know why? Because the word about Aaron was that he was a *stiff.* You'd hear people from the networks say, 'Trying to do anything with that guy is like watching grass grow.' "

"You always get it wrong, Foley," says Norm Lane. "What the guy said was 'like watching Astroturf grow.' "

Foley says, "The Gillette commercial made a lot of people look at Hank Aaron as a human being for the first time and not just a base-hit robot. They saw him clowning around. They saw he had a sense of humor. They saw he had a personality, and on top of that he was honest. That commercial was a breakthrough, Willie. It was a breakthrough in our business, and it was a breakthrough for Henry Aaron. This isn't generally remembered, but it was right after that you started hearing Aaron referred to as a superstar."

Oh, those slippery pink little pimps. Before I knew it, they had me turned completely around. They *had* me. All I expected from the commercial in the first place was a miracle . . . and these two pimps give me a goddamn preview in living color!

AFTER THAT I LET THEM TAKE ME BACK OUT ONTO THE SET. *Let* them, if you get the picture. I was feeling used, trifled with, but they *had* me. I really *wanted* the goddamned commercial now.

Shooting the thing was pure hell. I'd say a few words, and the director would say, "Cut," and he'd say, "Now, this time, Willie, just relax," or he'd say, "Have fun with it." Have fun. The main thing on my mind was to pronounce every word exactly right, so that when I got to the Charlie Magnet part, people couldn't help but know it was just a gag. I was laying those words down like tiles.

But they acted like I couldn't say anything right. They'd say, "All quiet! Speed! Roll it! Action!" "Cut!" and then "Take 9—Charlemagne Willie Hammer" and then "Take 10—Charlemagne Willie Hammer" and then it was getting up to "Take 24," "Take 25—Charlemagne Willie Hammer" and it was like they had this cripple on their hands. The man would have these breaks, and he'd take me off to one side again and tell me not to worry about the takes. He'd say the commercial only runs thirty seconds, but it always takes all day to shoot one. He'd say, "There's nothing wrong with you, Willie. Nobody expects you to be an actor, Willie." I knew what that code stuff meant.

We'd gotten up to about "Take 43—Charlemagne Willie Hammer" and I was just sitting there with my legs crossed, and this colored kid I was mentioning before comes onto the set and he says, "Hey, man!" and he give me a wink and he kneels down and takes out a little penknife and he scrapes something off the bottom of my shoe and hands it to me. It's a price sticker! It says "Saks Fifth Avenue" in little letters at the top and "$87.50" at the bottom. The kid points his finger and he says, "I gotcha covered."

And *two people laughed!* And then I knew! All day long, out in the shadows, in the gloom, on the rigs—all day long these bastards had been goofing off my brand-new McAfee shoes: "Another cotton chopper's caught the bus to New York City!"

We said goodbye to "Take 50—Charlemagne Willie Hammer." We were down at the part where I say, "You know . . . I think I'll TRY it!"—and then I'm supposed to break into my big laugh. I couldn't get that laugh out. It wouldn't come. There was no way I could make it come. I would get to the point where I was supposed to laugh . . . and I could hear these terrible sounds coming out of my own mouth. I was braying, I was moaning, I was baying at the lights . . . The bastards . . . a chuckle over here, a snort back over there . . .

"Action!" "Cut!" "Take 55—Charlemagne Willie Hammer," and I mean I'm struggling out here under these goddamn lights, and one more time I say, "You know . . . I think I'll TRY it!"—and one more time nothing but some kind of miserable croak comes out.

"Cut!" "Take 56—Charlemagne Willie Hammer," "Action!" and one more time I'm saying "You know . . . I think I'll TRY

it!"—and one more time I'm wondering what kind of fool noise
I'm gonna make on this try—when all of a sudden I hear this
voice crying out:

"Hey, Willie! Your fly's open!"

Hunh—a *tornado!* My eyes keel over! I'm checking out the lap
of my $400 gabardine suit! I know I'm gonna see it! . . . the final
piece of shit! . . . the *gaping fly!* . . . They're gonna use it! they
gonna make their *break*through! . . . into a hundred million
homes with the gates open for a willie hammer! . . . My brain's
catching up . . . Hey, sucker, that voice . . . it's *Foley's!* . . . your
fly's not open, sucker, you're just a poor jerk out here in the spotlight in New York City . . . goosed by the fat boy for all to see! . . .
I'm relieved . . . I'm embarrassed . . . I'm mocked . . . I'm *had* . . .
It all rushes together in my belly . . . It cries out for air . . . I hear
it coming up from out of my boyhood . . . the sound of the sucker
who's got himself made fool of again . . . the sound of the most
pitiful jerk that ever got dumped on in the high-school locker
room! . . . the sound of the goosy lucy who gets the joke too
late . . . the sound of the fat bubba with his head caught in the
bummer . . . the last living cry of surrender of all the sad-ass
suckers, dull tools, hopeless fools, and natural-born flaming nut-
balls of this world . . . What I'm saying is: I laughed.

That laugh came from down so deep, from out of such a deep
well of shame, in such a gush, it stopped everything cold. It was
like thirty or forty people in the giant gloom, out on the rigs,
sucked in their breath at once—and then suddenly the man was
jumping up in the air and throwing his conked hair around and
yelling:

"Beautiful! It's a wrap, Willie! You're my baby!"

—and then the whole goddamn place caves in on me—it's like
one huge laugh cracks out from the monster . . . from one and
all . . . they're gasping . . . they're weeping . . . racking their
guts . . . squalling like babies . . . The man must see the look in
my face . . . He's no fool . . . he's ready to scram . . . he's telling me:

"No kidding, Willie. That's beautiful! I'm serious! Oh, Jesus!"

He's biting on the sleeve of his blue-jean jacket to keep from laughing . . . He has a mouthful . . .

Foley's saying, "Goddamn! You're a good sport, Willie!"

He's no fool, either . . . he's moving off, him and Norm Lane, talking over their shoulders . . . Everybody's moving around . . . trying not to look at me . . . laughing their asses off, weeping, snuffling, shaking their heads . . . It's like steam has gone off in my head . . . *Just get the hell outta here, man!* No, I hung on to my Plan. So help me. I came into this place in the morning with the duffel bag full of bats and balls and I gave them to one and all like the Santa Claus of the big league, and that was so when the job was done, I could hit these people up for two or three cases of Charlemagne cologne and shaving cream and after-shave lotion and come walking back into the clubhouse in the Astrodome and hand this stuff out to the ballplayers and say, "Yeah, they gave me all this stuff to give you guys. Help yourselves." And they'd get the message the cool way. They'd say, "Goddamn, Hammer got a commercial. That sucker's got the superstar thing going!"

But could a man like me really be in such a sorry state . . . and could a crocodile like me really turn into such a hummingbird, that after getting jerked around and humped over the way they had done it to me, I could really walk up to Foley and ask for a goddamn shitload of Charlemagne? The answer is . . . a man can sink that low! A man can lose that much self-respect! The supply is run out! . . . It's leaked clean away . . . There's nothing left but Vanity! There's just a goldfish flopping on the table! With thirty seconds left!

That was how come I make for the door on the side. Hey, Foley! It opens onto a stairwell. They're in there. The sound of those two pimps hits me like the biggest gob of spit in the history of the world. Those two fat pimps were up against the wall, by a fire extinguisher, laughing like goddamn crazy people.

Foley's back is to me, but Norm Lane can see me. His little eyes open like "This is the Last Day." Willie Hammer is going to be giving the lecture now! I move toward Foley, but just to tap

him on the shoulder and spin him around—I swear that's all!—
my fist wasn't even closed! ... I try to move toward him ... My
damn foot slips! ... My damn brand-new McAfees ... they're
like ice! ... Foley has halfway turned his head ... he's got a look
on his face like Norm Lane ... He's done for! He's mine! He's
finished! He's seen the eye! He's a spot of grease! He's a moth
hole! ... But shit, I'm sinking ... It's eternity and no time at all!
I'm sinking and Foley's shooting up in the air! ... I can't believe
it! ... I'm falling on my ass!

And that's when I cracked my head against the wall. So help
me, I wasn't knocked out. I was only stunned. I slipped. I don't
care what lies the sucker tells. People like him have themselves to
live with. Like the Bible says, "When he speaketh a lie, he
speaketh of his own: for he is a liar, and the father of it."

AFTER MY LITTLE SET-TO WITH WILLIE HAMMER, NORM LANE
started calling me the White Hope. He called me that over a
thousand lunches in every American Express mess hall in the
East Fifties. That and the "Schwartze Patrol" and "Captain Midnight." Norm Lane happens to be one of those people who think
that because they were born Jewish, the ordinary polite conver-
sational racial regulations are suspended. If I said a tenth of the
things he says all the time about Jews and blacks, he'd be shocked
out of his pants.

I don't know ... I may be too sensitive about it, but I've always
had the feeling that in New York, in our business, the Irishman
has to keep proving he's Enlightened. I could be wrong, but that's
the way I feel. You aren't exactly presumed to be a bigot—nothing so gross as that—you're just presumed to have a calloused
sensibility. You're presumed to be a cop in a business suit. Neat
and sweet-smelling—but still a flatfoot! So you feel like you have
to pray in public a lot, to Peace, Art, Equality, and Good Taste,
pray out loud for all to hear ... wear a little Dr. Scholl's on your
soul ... Leaving the *Daily News* aside, which isn't all that hard to

do—the press, television, advertising, show business, the arts, are a club for Jews and Protestants. I swear to God, an Irishman is a rarity! an exotic!—and I grew up thinking the Irish ran New York City. I was only wrong by about forty years. I finally reached New York, out of college, and all our boys had was the Police Department, the Fire Department, a couple of unions that didn't bear public mention after sunup, the *Daily News,* Representative Charles Buckley of the Bronx, and Cardinal Spellman giving a Christmas message from the U.S.O. on Lexington Avenue. What a grim slide! I think the Armenians and Turks are in better shape! The Turks have Ahmet Ertegun!

Well, I'll tell you one thing that Norm Lane and all my other Jewish and Waspo pals managed to forget after the Willie Hammer business. It so happens that I am one of the few people in advertising who has gone out of his way within the industry itself for black people. The fact is, I stuck my big vilified Irish neck out for Willie Hammer!

The Fabrilex account was only the biggest thing in my career. So I chose that moment for one of my fits of Enlightenment... Fabrilex is the old American Elastic Fabric Company, which made girdles. After the Second World War they expanded into a big line of female health and beauty aids and became Fabrilex. And now they were making their next great leap, moving into men's toiletries with the Charlemagne line, with an advertising budget of ten million dollars. That's about par for a new line of that sort. It was not something that happened every day with our agency, however. Our cut was 15 percent, or one and a half million dollars. When I was named the account executive for the campaign, that was big news. People sent me cards.

My opposite number at Fabrilex was a horrible grim Waspo bastard named Wynn Sprague. He has one of those English noses you could shave roast beef with. He's a real Mr. Transistors. He doesn't laugh, he just grins and lets the noise on the loop come out. Sprague is their vice-president in charge of advertising and one of the four or five big men in the bunker.

Like any corporation with half a brain among its assets and the desire to unload a few billion dollars' worth of Closet Queen ointment on the American male, Fabrilex wanted to introduce the Charlemagne line with jock commercials. They wanted to introduce all their sweet things in the spike-bending paws of the most supervirile superstars in the world of sports. The budget for the twelve jock commercials for Charlemagne cologne was $500,000.

So far, the usual . . . and then the Enlightened Irishman had to step in. Sprague and the Fabrilex people didn't have the faintest desire to include a black athlete in the series. They knew, as everybody knows, that endorsements by black celebrities only move merchandise among black people. But more to the point, they turn off a lot of whites; and the more personal the product, the greater the risk. In Cincinnati, Ohio, at Fabrilex Central, the appeal of putting Charlemagne into the sturdy mitts of Willie Hammer or any other black man might be described, using a scale of from one to ten, as at about minus 740. So why couldn't the Enlightened Irishman leave well enough alone?

Here we get back to praying in public and allied matters. I do, in fact, believe that advertising is no longer the Big Con, the "Madison Avenue" of the late forties and early fifties. There's no reason why advertising can't have a conscience and a sense of responsibility. As a matter of fact, it is only because a few of us feel that way that you now see any black faces in network advertising at all. It has nothing to do with marketing and demographics—believe me—and even less to do with the goodwill of the manufacturers. The entire push has come from inside the agencies in New York, and I've done my share.

I can remember the arguments with Sprague and his gimlet deacons very well. I'd bring out the statistics: nineteen of the leading thirty hitters in baseball were black. Almost all the great running backs and offensive ends in football were black. Sixty-five percent of the players in professional basketball were black. It was not realistic to run a big advertising campaign featuring professional athletes and not include a single black man. "Realistic" was the word I chose, but it was essentially a moral argument and cut no ice in Cincinnati . . . until I mentioned the Possible Protests. Quite a few organizations, such as B.L.A.S.T. (Black and Latin Alliance for Soul Talent), were beginning to agitate about the absence of black faces in all phases of television. I don't know whether it was the thirty-story monument that Fabrilex had just built to itself in pulse-quickening downtown Cincinnati, a prodigious office complex that nobody wanted to move into . . . and all they needed now was a mob of raving black militants picketing out front and they'd really have a gone elephant on their hands . . . or whether it was the sneaking fear that the merciless Zulus might creep out into suburban Morley Heights to continue their vicious work by night . . . a little tinkling of the glass in the French doors of the Sprague manse, a twist of the knob . . . and *Uhuru! Mamba Jabba Zabba! Gee-dum!* . . . the whole mob pouring in, bones through their noses, crazy for spareribs . . . In any event, Sprague gave in. One blackamoor would be okay.

It is at this point, after the first hurdle, that the Enlightened Irishman must have not only high ideals but fancy little dancing feet. What he must avoid at all costs is choosing the athlete who looks like the Black Threat. That's why a fine gentleman and great athlete like Willie Stargell of the Pirates is never chosen. Millions of white men watching him hit home runs for the Pittsburgh Pirates see a black man who looks about seven feet tall and who doesn't prime himself for the pitcher's delivery in the accepted fashion, which is by wiggling your ass and your bat a little bit. No, he whomps the bat overhead toward the pitcher like an ax or a sledgehammer, as if he's ready to pound him into the ground feet first. That's why the token black jock is so often a Grand Old Man, on the safe side of forty, like Willie Mays or Hank Aaron.

Willie Hammer appealed to the Enlightened Irishman precisely because he wasn't the solid safe old man. Hammer was young, he had just come into his own, he was leading the National League in hitting by forty-five points, and in every picture he looked lean, powerful, and yet handsome in a way that verged on the delicate, somewhat like Vida Blue or Rod Carew. The agents who usually knew about prominent athletes, such as the people at Mattgo, knew little about Willie Hammer. So we did what you do in such cases. We sounded out his club's p.-r. man, a man named Connie Fisher. You approach the p.-r. man on an insider-to-insider basis, as one media sophisticate to another. You say, "I'm sure you understand the things we need to know, and it'll be absolutely confidential." They'll usually level with you. They're flattered as hell, of course.

"Willie's okay in my book," Mr. Connie Fisher said, "but he doesn't say much. There were some guys here from NBC interested in Willie for a Black Stars special they were thinking about. One of them said, 'I've been hanging around that guy for a week now. It's like watching Astroturf grow.' That broke me up. The other one said, 'Willie Hammer. Good hit, no spiel.' "

"Well," I said, "what's his basic personality? Is he . . . does he strike you as . . . surly or . . ."

"You mean is he a Bad Mother?"

I was so high-minded, I despised the man for using such an expression . . . although, in fact, he was putting into words exactly what was up in my towering ivory cortex.

"Oh hell, no," he said. "Willie's a gentleman through and through. He's basically conservative. He likes to live well. He has a beautiful home out in Bayou Grove, which is the black gold coast here, I suppose you'd say. He has a beautiful wife, light-skinned, and I think she's active in the Southern Christian Leadership Conference. Willie isn't active in politics at all, as far as I know. Willie likes good clothes, and I'm not talking about Scarlet Creeper pimp clothes and all that. He goes to the most expensive tailor in Houston. There's not a box-holder at the Astrodome who can hold a candle to the man. Not that I'm saying this is the world's greatest center of refinement. Hog-stomping baroque goes over just fine here. But Willie is pretty as a picture by any-body's standards, black or white. In fact, I think that's Willie's main problem. He doesn't know whether he's black or white."

Norm didn't think Willie Hammer sounded like any great ball of fire. But he had some check marks, too. He was good-looking, something of a fashion plate, even. That was always something to think about in a jock commercial for men's per-fume, because they're always done in street clothes. The idea in a men's-perfume commercial is not the locker-room crusade against B.O.... The idea is, going out and cutting just colossal freaking mountains of ice with the ladies.

What really sold me, I must confess, was the name ... Willie Hammer ... I swear to God, was there ever a more perfect name for a baseball player! I kept thinking of Dick Butkus. As a per-sonality in TV commercials, Butkus was a stiff, a cipher, a nul-lity. But the appearance of the man! He came rolling in front of the camera like a hill. And inside of this behemoth was a squeaky little voice, which somehow made it better. And my God, the name!—a goat the size of a rhinoceros!—what the hell else *could* he be but the greatest middle linebacker in the history of foot-ball? He didn't need a personality. He might have rolled over on it in his sleep. And that was the way I started thinking about Willie Hammer. Willie Hammer! Willie Hammer! It was a Buf-falo Bayou two-beat!

In fact, I didn't start getting the clanks until Norm and I fi-nally met Willie in New York and took him over to the Palm the night before the shooting. My boy was ... *a* ... *stiff*! He seemed so out of it that right away Norm and I got the same idea: he was such a country boy that the Palm might be a letdown. We always take our jock stars to some famous trencherman's steak house, like Gallagher's or Stampler's or the Palm, and I think the Palm is the best. But the sight of it doesn't exactly say City Lights. So all the way over in the cab we kept saying, "Well, it's a little weird-looking ... but they've got *fabulous steaks*."

Willie had nothing to say all night. He acted like Eastern had checked his head through to Montreal. On the other hand, he came walking into the Palm looking like a million dollars . . . except that he had some kind of weird trick thing he kept doing with his neck, and people were kind of staring at it. Norm and I were burning out the ignition just trying to keep the conversation going with the guy. Norm finally got off onto one of his Jewish forced marches, about women's liberation and castration obsessions and, Christ, I don't know, the worst load of cod you can imagine—it embarrassed me, although I have to admit *I* didn't know how you reached the man. But he *looked* good! And he was still named Willie Hammer, all night long!

By the time we got to X.T.O. the next morning, the Enlightened Irishman was very much on edge. Our shootings so far had not exactly delighted the Client, meaning Sprague. I detested the son of a bitch, but he wasn't stupid. He knew what he was getting. Nolan Perry and Brook Howard had been only fair. Tommy Cash had been a disaster. I wasn't even sure we could use what we shot. Tommy Cash is one of those garrulous country boys who has a big red barn full of cornball personality in an ordinary conversation. In front of the camera he just congealed. The only part of his personality that was left was that he didn't know what he'd said from one second to the next. Well, at least Willie's entry was encouraging. He completely surprised me by turning up with a duffel bag full of bats and balls. He won Sprague over right away. This was a *very* good sign in my book, because during a shooting there are two kinds of Client. The Class A Client is a lamb. He gives you your head. He may not like what you're doing, but he doesn't butt in on the set. The Class B Client is a Sprague. He's got his nose into everything. I've seen guys like that stop a whole shooting and tell you to scrap it. One of the sad facts of life is that the Client is the Law west of the Pecos. Somehow Willie had slipped a training muzzle over the Client right away.

So when Willie suddenly balked—right off the top—without a word of warning—I was freaking dumbfounded. There was Willie out in the middle of the set saying *Naw.* I must confess that many vile thoughts bubbled up into my brain. "Goddamn it, Willie, don't you turn into the Bad Mother on me! Don't you turn into the pseudo-ignorant malingering darky on my time—"

But I swear to Christ, in the next moment I was filled with the most overpowering pity and guilt. The man was obviously in some kind of anguish. And he was *alone* out there under the lights. He didn't even have an agent along. All at once the sight of his elegant suit and his new shoes with the spanking-tan soles and the goddamned price sticker still on them—it was so *touching* that I can't describe it to you. All of a sudden I was just looking at a poor black guy who had made his way in the world as best he could. I was halfway on the verge of walking out there and saying, "Okay, Willie, let's just call it off."

Well . . . that's not quite entirely true, is it, Irishman? You were sweating . . . you could feel the chilly breath . . . Sprague didn't even bother to whisper. The Client doesn't have to bother. "What's wrong with the man?" he kept saying, as if I'd foisted off a horse with the heaves on him.

I was praying that Marshall Lewis, our director, could pull the thing out quickly. Marshall is a very sensitive guy—but, then, all the directors in TV commercials are very sensitive, come to think of it, *artists,* you understand—it's only people like Fellini and Antonioni who sit around talking about money and cars—but, anyway, Marshall has always been very good with celebrities who aren't actors. Marshall's basic technique is to create a creek of sympathy that is so wet and so deep that he and the performer go washing down it together, buddies against the elements. But he's also a bit soft. I knew that the only thing that was going to turn Willie around was to get tough. Well, hell, I guess I was really trying to protect myself in front of Sprague. I had to look *in charge.* Ordinarily this would have been Norm's problem, as agency producer, but I wasn't leaving anything to the Charming Flake. Sprague was standing there now saying things like, "He's *your* inspiration, Foley," as if to say, "If this one goes under, Butterfingers, this is the last ship you'll ever sail."

I didn't even know what the hell I was going to say to Willie. All I had figured out was a tone. I looked stern. I turned my palms up toward heaven, exactly the way the priests used to do it. It wasn't me who pulled it out, however. It was Norm. He saw the key as soon as Willie mentioned Hank Aaron: if Aaron could go out and make this kind of commercial, then Willie could do it. Of course, then we got pretty outrageous about the whole thing. The whole bit about how they said covering Aaron was "like watching Astroturf grow"—that was what they said about Willie himself! We were really rotten bastards! We were describing Willie Hammer in the bluntest possible terms, right to his face, and calling it "Hank Aaron"!

The shooting was dreadful, just dreadful. Willie started saying the lines with the most incredible prissiness. He sounded like Martin Luther King—Martin Luther King orating in slang about a men's perfume.

The goddamn Sprague was having fits. "Foley, Foley, Foley, Foley" was his chant all afternoon. It was too much like the liturgy of interment to make the jolly Irishman feel very good. I caved in, friends! You bet! I looked after Foley very well! I cranked up my quivering guts, resolved to save the day for Charlemagne, Fabrilex, Mr. Wynn Sprague, and downtown Cincinnati.

Seeing Willie out there trying to laugh was the brutal final touch. You never heard such sounds in your life. Sometimes he sounded like an owl, an owl with intestinal flu, out in the middle of Interstate 95. Everybody was bleeding for the guy. I could hear stagehands clearing their throats out of their own agony for the man. But did the Enlightened Irishman's heart bleed? No longer. He had replaced it around 4:30 p.m. He was 100 percent Mr. Transistors himself now, ready to play all data as it lay. I didn't think up "Your fly's open." The computer did it. The digits made me do it. It just popped into my brain. But when it worked—well, I mean, it was a genuinely funny moment. The whole X.T.O. Teletronics crew collapsed. Relief, weariness, sheer off-the-wall wackiness—they just broke up. It was just as funny as hell for about five seconds ... until you saw what was on Willie Hammer's face. I beat a fast retreat. I ducked out the fire exit with Norm Lane, but the goddamned Norm got me laughing all over again. And that was when Willie suddenly appeared.

He was 185 pounds of trouble from top to bottom. He was the red dragon in the Book of Revelation with fire coming out of its eyes. He didn't say a word—he swung on me!

Now, in that kind of moment, things happen or they don't. I haven't kept myself in top shape, although I used to play a little ball, at the University of Massachusetts, and I guess I've never really been out of shape. I did the only thing I could do. I slipped his punch and I hit him. I hit him with my fist, or maybe it was my forearm. Norm can't remember, either. His version is a blur, another little belch of the Lane laughing gas.

Anyway—the poor guy was out cold!

It's curious, the things that stick in your mind at such a time. He was laid out flat on his face and I could see the soles of his shoes and they were as bright and clean as a brand-new varnished pine board. Out of the blue, something popped into my head, something I hadn't thought about in thirty years, not since the time when I was a kid and my folks took me to the cathedral to see the ordination of a prior, and the good brother laid himself out prostrate on the floor of the sanctuary, and his head pointed toward the altar and the Powers that be and his feet pointed toward all of us—and the soles of his shoes were snow-white! immaculate! As if he were pure and walked only on clouds! It seemed like the most marvelous thing! But why was he lying there? What had he done to God?

THE INCIDENT NEVER SAW PRINT ANYWHERE, DESPITE THE liveliest rumors. Both men were resolute about denying all. The black athlete, for reasons of pride. The advertising executive, so as not to jeopardize the biggest account of his career. The matter of the Fallen Star would have made jolly reading, but not in Transistorsville.

In the long run, however, the advertising executive did not find the incident at all hard to live with. The story had the most extraordinary appeal. Via word of mouth, he became a legend in the industry. In no time he was president of his agency, handled 10-million-dollar accounts galore, set himself such a salary they drew straws for him down at the Church Street I.R.S., was named co-chairman of a national foundation promoting Black Culture, won many scrolls and plaques in the Brotherhood line, ascended to the board of one of the most prestigious museums in New York, was photographed standing beside his gutsy (the decorator's term) new seventeenth-century refectory table for *Town & Country* as an ornament of the Cultural World.

As for the black athlete, the commercial was anything but a disaster. The incredible pomposity of his delivery, followed by a laugh that seemed like a propane explosion in the solar plexus, was taken as evidence of a natural-born comedian. It was one of those commercials that people repeat lines from. He became known as a personality and, in due time, as a superstar. He returned from his New York trip with the scales lifted from his eyes. He began to Come Back, as the saying goes, to Speak Out, to Lead, and, for the first time, to be Black Enough. He said he guessed he had merely needed a chance to get away by himself and think. A term he coined, "the Ritz cracker," entered the language. His wife fell in love with him. Civil-rights leaders never failed to look him up when they were in town. Businessmen courted him and steered him to several million dollars in a short time. He appeared at a White House dinner in a set of tails of which his tailor was publicly proud (in *Stitcher & Cutter*), and the President remarked on his uncommonly dry sense of humor.

The Spirit of the Age
(and what it longs for)

chapter V

The Intelligent Coed's
Guide to America

1. O'Hare!

OMOTHER O'HARE, BIG BOSOM FOR OUR HUNGRY POETS, pelvic saddle for our sexologists and Open Classroom theorists—O houri O'Hare, who keeps her Perm-O-Pour Stoneglow thighs ajar to receive a generation of frustrated and unreadable novelists—

But wait a minute. It may be too early for the odes. Has it even been duly noted that O'Hare, which is an airport outside Chicago, is now the intellectual center of the United States?

Curious, but true. There at O'Hare, on any day, Monday through Friday, from September to June, they sit . . . in row after Mies van der row of black vinyl and stainless-steel sling chairs . . . amid soaring walls of plate glass . . . from one tenth to one third of the literary notables of the United States. In October and April, the peak months, the figure goes up to one half.

Masters and Johnson and Erica Jong, Kozol and Rifkin and

Hacker and Kael, Steinem and Nader, Marks, Hayden and Mailer, Galbraith and Heilbroner, and your bear-market brothers in the PopEco business, Lekachman & Others—which of you has not hunkered down lately in the prodigious lap of Mother O'Hare!

And why? Because they're heading out into the land to give lectures. They are giving lectures at the colleges and universities of America's heartland, which runs from Fort Lee, New Jersey, on the east to the Hollywood Freeway on the west. Giving lectures in the heartland is one of the lucrative dividends of being a noted writer in America. It is the writer's faint approximation of, say, Joe Cocker's $25,000 one-night stand at the West Springfield Fair. All the skyways to Lectureland lead through O'Hare Airport. In short, up to one half of our intellectual establishment sits outside of Chicago between planes.

At a literary conference at Notre Dame, I (no stranger to bountiful O'Hare myself) ran into a poet who is noted for his verse celebrating the ecology, née Nature. He lives in a dramatic house nailed together completely from uncut pieces of hickory driftwood, perched on a bluff overlooking the crashing ocean, a spot so remote that you can drive no closer than five miles to it by conventional automobile and barely within a mile and a half by Jeep. The last 7,500 feet it's hand over hand up rocks, vines, and lengths of hemp. I remarked that this must be the ideal setting in which to write about the ecological wonders.

"I wouldn't know," he said. "I do all my writing in O'Hare."

And what is the message that the bards and sages of O'Hare bring to millions of college students in the vast fodderlands of the nation? I'm afraid I must report that it is a gloomy message; morose, even, heading for gangrene.

2. The Frisbee ion

If you happen to attend a conference at which whole contingents of the O'Hare philosophers assemble, you can get the message in

The lost coed Cunégonde

all its varieties in a short time. Picture, if you will, a university on the Great Plains . . . a new Student Activities Center the color of butter-almond ice cream . . . a huge interior space with tracks in the floor, along which janitors in green twill pull Expando-Flex accordion walls to create meeting rooms of any size. The conference is about to begin. The students come surging in like hormones. You've heard of rosy cheeks? They *have* them! Here they come, rosy-cheeked, laughing, with Shasta and 7-Up pumping through their veins, talking chipsy, flashing weatherproof smiles, bursting out of their down-filled Squaw Valley jackets and their blue jeans—O immortal denim mons veneris!—looking, all of them, boys and girls, Jocks & Buds & Freaks, as if they spent the day hang-gliding and then made a Miller commercial at dusk and are now going to taper off with a little Culture before returning to the coed dorm. They grow quiet. The conference begins. The keynote speaker, a historian wearing a calfskin jacket and hair like Felix Mendelssohn's, informs them that the United States is "a leaden, life-denying society."

Over the next thirty-six hours, other O'Hare regulars fill in the rest:

Sixty families control one half the private wealth of America, and two hundred corporations own two thirds of the means of production. "A small group of nameless, faceless men" who avoid publicity the way a werewolf avoids the dawn now dominates American life. In America a man's home is not his castle but merely "a gigantic listening device with a mortgage"—a reference to eavesdropping by the FBI and the CIA. America's foreign policy has been and continues to be based upon war, assassination, bribery, genocide, and the sabotage of democratic governments. "The new McCarthyism" (Joe's, not Gene's) is already upon us. Following a brief charade of free speech, the "gagging of the press" has resumed. Racism in America has not diminished; it is merely more subtle now. The gulf between rich and poor widens daily, creating "permanent ghetto-colonial populations." The decline in economic growth is causing a crisis in capitalism, which will lead shortly to authoritarian rule and to a new America in which everyone waits, in horror, for the knock on the door in the dead of the night, the descent of the knout on the nape of the neck—

HOW OTHER PEOPLE ATTENDING THIS CONFERENCE FELT BY now, I didn't dare ask. As for myself, I was beginning to feel like Job or Miss Cunégonde. What further devastations or humiliations could possibly be in store, short of the sacking of Kansas City? It was in that frame of mind that I attended the final panel discussion, which was entitled "The United States in the Year 2000."

The prognosis was not good, as you can imagine. But I was totally unprepared for the astounding news brought by an ecologist.

"I'm not sure I want to be alive in the year 2000," he said, although he certainly looked lively enough at the moment. He was about thirty-eight, and he wore a Madras plaid cotton jacket and a Disco Magenta turtleneck jersey.

It seemed that recent studies showed that, due to the rape of the atmosphere by aerosol spray users, by 2000 a certain ion would no longer be coming our way from the sun. I can't remember which one . . . the aluminum ion, the magnesium ion, the neon ion, the gadolinium ion, the calcium ion . . . the calcium ion perhaps; in any event, it was crucial for the formation of bones, and by 2000 it would be no more. Could such a thing be? Somehow this went beyond any of the horrors I was already imagining. I began free-associating . . . Suddenly I could see Lexington Avenue, near where I live in Manhattan. The presence of the storm troopers was the least of it. It was the look of ordinary citizens that was so horrible. Their bones were going. They were dissolving. Women who had once been clicking and clogging down the avenue up on five-inch platform soles, with their pants seams smartly cleaving their declivities, were now mere denim &

patent-leather blobs . . . oozing and inching and suppurating along the sidewalk like amoebas or ticks . . . A cab driver puts his arm out the window . . . and it just dribbles down the yellow door like hot Mazola . . . A blind news dealer tries to give change to a notions buyer for Bloomingdale's, and their fingers run together like fettucine over a stack of *New York Post*s . . . It's horrible . . . it's obscene . . . it's the end—

I was so dazed, I was no longer wondering what the assembled students thought of all this. But just at that moment one of them raised his hand. He was a tall boy with a lot of curly hair and a Fu Manchu mustache.

"Yes?" said the ecologist.

"There's one thing I can't understand," said the boy.

"What's that?" said the ecologist.

"Well," said the boy. "I'm a senior, and for four years we've been told by people like yourself and the other gentlemen that everything's in terrible shape, and it's all going to hell, and I'm willing to take your word for it, because you're all experts in your fields. But around here, at this school, for the past four years, the biggest problem, as far as I can see, has been finding a parking place near the campus."

Dead silence. The panelists looked at this poor turkey to try to size him up. Was he trying to be funny? Or was this the native bray of the heartland? The ecologist struck a note of forbearance as he said:

"I'm sure that's true, and that illustrates one of the biggest difficulties we have in making realistic assessments. A university like this, after all, is a middle-class institution, and middle-class life is calculated precisely to create a screen—"

"I understand all that," said the boy. "What I want to know is—how old are you, usually, when it all hits you?"

And suddenly the situation became clear. The kid was no wiseacre! He was genuinely perplexed! . . . For four years he had been squinting at the horizon . . . looking for the grim horrors which he knew—on faith—to be all around him . . . and had been utterly unable to find them . . . and now he was afraid they might descend on him all at once when he least expected it. He might be walking down the street in Omaha one day, minding his own business, when—whop! whop! whop! whop!—War! Fascism! Repression! Corruption!—they'd squash him like bowling balls rolling off a roof!

Who was that lost lad? What was his name? Without knowing it, he was playing the xylophone in a boneyard. He was the unique new creature of the 1970's. He was Candide in reverse. Candide and Miss Cunégonde, one will recall, are taught by an all-knowing savant, Dr. Pangloss. He keeps assuring them that this is "the best of all possible worlds," and they believe him implicitly—even though their lives are one catastrophe after another. Now something much weirder was happening. The Jocks & Buds & Freaks of the heartland have their all-knowing savants of O'Hare, who keep warning them that this is "the worst of all possible worlds," and they know it must be true—and yet life keeps getting easier, sunnier, happier . . . *Frisbee!*

How can such things be?

3. S-s-s-s-s-s-ssssssss

One Saturday night in 1965 I found myself on a stage at Princeton University with Günter Grass, Allen Ginsberg, Paul Krassner, and an avant-garde filmmaker named Gregory Markopoulos. We were supposed to talk about "the style of the sixties." The auditorium had a big balcony and a lot of moldings. It reminded me of the National Opera House in San José, Costa Rica. The place was packed with about twelve hundred Princeton students and their dates. Before things got started, it was hard to figure out just what they expected. Somebody up in the balcony kept making a sound like a baby crying. Somebody on the main floor always responded with a strange sound he was able to make with his mouth and his cupped hands. It sounded like a raccoon trapped in a garbage can. The baby . . . the raccoon in a can . . . Every time they did it the whole place cracked up, twelve hundred Princeton students and their dates. "Dates" . . . yes . . . this was back before the era of "Our eyes met, our lips met, our bodies met, and then we were introduced."

Anyway, the format was that each man on the stage would make an opening statement about the 1960's, and then the panel discussion would begin. Günter Grass, as Germany's new giant of the novel, the new Thomas Mann, went first. He understood English but didn't feel confident speaking in English, and so he made his statement in German. I doubt that there were ten people in the place who knew what he was saying, but he seemed to speak with gravity and passion. When he finished, there was tremendous applause. Then an interpreter named Albert Harrison (as I recall) delivered Mr. Grass's remarks in English. Sure enough, they were grave and passionate. They were about the responsibility of the artist in a time of struggle and crisis. The applause was even greater than before. Some of the students rose to their feet. Some of the dates rose, too.

The moderator was Paul Krassner, editor of *The Realist* magazine. I remember looking over at Krassner. He looked like one of the trolls that live under the bridge in Norse tales and sit there stroking their molting noses and waiting for hotshots to swagger over the span. Krassner had to wait for about two minutes for the applause to die down enough to make himself heard. Then he leaned into his microphone and said quite solemnly:

"Thank you, Günter Grass. And thank you, Albert Harrison, for translating . . . Mr. Grass's bar mitzvah speech."

Stunned—like twelve hundred veal calves entering the abattoir. Then came the hissing. Twelve hundred Princeton students & dates started hissing. I had never heard such a sound before . . . an entire hall consumed in hisses . . .

"S-s-s-s-s-s-s-s-s-ssssssss!"

You couldn't hear yourself talk. You could only hear that sibilant storm. Krassner just sat there with his manic-troll look on, waiting for it to die down. It seemed to take forever. When the storm began to subside a bit, he leaned into the microphone again and said:

"For two years I've been hearing that God is dead. I'm very much relieved to see he only sprung a leak."

For some reason, that stopped the hissing. The kid up in the balcony made a sound like a baby crying. The kid on the main floor made a sound like a raccoon in a garbage can. The crowd laughed and booed, and people tried out new noises. The gyroscope was now gone from the control panel . . . Our trajectory was end over end . . .

The next thing I knew, the discussion was onto the subject of fascism in America. Everybody was talking about police repression and the anxiety and paranoia as good folks waited for the knock on the door and the descent of the knout on the nape of the neck. I couldn't make any sense out of it. I had just made a tour of the country to write a series called "The New Life Out There" for *New York* magazine. This was the mid-1960's. The post–World War II boom had by now pumped money into every level of the population on a scale unparalleled in any nation in history. Not only that, the folks were running wilder and freer than any people in history. For that matter, Krassner himself, in one of the strokes of exuberance for which he was well known, was soon to publish a slight hoax: an account of how Lyndon Johnson was so overjoyed about becoming President that he had buggered a wound in the neck of John F. Kennedy on Air Force One as Kennedy's body was being flown back from Dallas. Krassner presented this as a suppressed chapter from William Manchester's book *Death of a President.* Johnson, of course, was still President when it came out. Yet the merciless gestapo dragnet missed Krassner, who cleverly hid out onstage at Princeton on Saturday nights.

Suddenly I heard myself blurting out over my microphone: "My God, what are you talking about? We're in the middle of a . . . Happiness Explosion!"

That merely sounded idiotic. The kid up in the balcony did

the crying baby. The kid down below did the raccoon . . . *Kraka-toa, East of Java* . . . I disappeared in a tidal wave of rude sounds . . . Back to the goon squads, search-and-seize and roust-a-daddy . . .

Support came from a quarter I hadn't counted on. It was Grass, speaking in English.

"For the past hour I have my eyes fixed on the doors here," he said. "You talk about fascism and police repression. In Germany when I was a student, they come through those doors long ago. Here they must be very slow."

Grass was enjoying himself for the first time all evening. He was not simply saying, "You really don't have so much to worry about." He was indulging his sense of the absurd. He was saying: "You American intellectuals—you want so desperately to feel besieged and persecuted!"

He sounded like Jean-François Revel, a French socialist writer who talks about one of the great unexplained phenomena of modern astronomy: namely, that the dark night of fascism is always descending in the United States and yet lands only in Europe.

Not very nice, Günter! Not very nice, Jean-François! A bit supercilious, wouldn't you say!

In fact, during the 1960's American intellectuals seldom seemed to realize just how patronizing their European brethren were being. To the Europeans, American intellectuals were struggling so hard (yet once again) to be correct in ideology and in attitude . . . and they were *being* correct . . . impeccable, even—which was precisely what prompted the sniggers and the knowing looks. European intellectuals looked upon American intellectuals much the way English colonial officials used to look upon the swarthy locals who came forward with their Calcutta Toff Oxford accents or their Lagos Mayfair tailored clothes. It was so touching *(then why are you laughing?)* to see the natives try to *do it right*.

I happened to have been in a room in Washington in 1961

when a member of Nigeria's first Cabinet (after independence) went into a long lament about the insidious and seductive techniques the British had used over the years to domesticate his people.

"Just look at *me!*" he said, looking down at his own torso and flipping his hands toward his chest. "Look at this *suit!* A worsted suit on an African—and a *double-breasted waistcoat!*"

He said "double-breasted waistcoat" with the most shriveling self-contempt you can imagine.

"This is what they've done to me," he said softly. "I can't even do the High Life any more."

The High Life was a Low Rent Nigerian dance. He continued to stare down at the offending waistcoat, wondering where he'd left his soul, or his Soul, in any event.

Perhaps someday, if Mr. Bob Silvers's *Confessions* are published, we will read something similar. Silvers is co-editor of *The New York Review of Books*. His accent arrived mysteriously one day in a box from London. Intrigued, he slapped it into his mouth like a set of teeth. It seemed . . . *right.* He began signing up so many English dons to write for *The New York Review of Books* that wags began calling it *The London Review of Bores* and *Don & Grub Street.* He seemed to take this good-naturedly. But perhaps someday we will learn that Mr. Bob Silvers, too, suffered blue moods of the soul and stood in front of a mirror wiggling his knees, trying to jiggle his roots, wondering if his feet could ever renegotiate the Lindy or the Fish or the Hokey-Pokey.

4. Hell's Angels

O how faithfully our native intelligentsia has tried to . . . *do it right!* The model has not always been England. Not at all. Just as frequently it has been Germany or France or Italy or even (on the religious fringe) the Orient. In the old days—seventy-five-or-so years ago—the well-brought-up young intellectual was likely to be treated to a tour of Europe . . . we find Jane Addams recuperating from her malaise in London and Dresden . . . Lincoln Steffens going to college in Heidelberg and Munich . . . Mabel Dodge setting up house in Florence . . . Randolph Bourne discovering Germany's "charming villages" and returning to Bloomfield, New Jersey—*Bloomfield, New Jersey?*—which now "seemed almost too grotesquely squalid and frowsy to be true." The business of being an intellectual and the urge to set oneself apart from provincial life began to be indistinguishable. In July 1921 Harold Stearns completed his anthology called *Civilization in the United States*—a contradiction in terms, he hastened to note—and set sail for Europe. The "Lost Generation" adventure began. But what was the Lost Generation really? It was a post–Great War discount tour in which middle-class Americans, too, not just Bournes and Steffenses, could learn how to become European intellectuals; preferably French.

The European intellectual! What a marvelous figure! A brilliant cynic, dazzling, in fact, set like one of those Gustave Miklos Art Deco sculptures of polished bronze and gold against the smoking rubble of Europe after the Great War. The American intellectual did the best he could. He could position himself against a backdrop of . . . well, not exactly rubble . . . but of the booboisie, the Herd State, the United States of Puritanism, Philistinism, Boosterism, Greed, and the great Hog Wallow. It was certainly a *psychological* wasteland. For the next fifty years, from that time to this, with ever-increasing skill, the American intellectual would perform this difficult feat, which might be described as the Adjectival Catch Up. The European intellectuals have a real wasteland? Well, we have a psychological wasteland. They have real fascism? Well, we have social fascism (a favorite phrase of the 1930's, amended to "liberal fascism" in the 1960's). They have real poverty? Well, we have relative poverty (Michael Harrington's great Adjectival Catch Up of 1963). They have real genocide? Well, we have cultural genocide (i.e., what universities were guilty of in the late 1960's if they didn't have open-admissions policies for minority groups).

Well—all right! They were difficult, these one-and-a-half gainers in logic. But they were worth it. What had become important above all was to be that polished figure amid the rubble, a vision of sweetness and light in the smoking tar pit of hell. The intellectual had become not so much an occupational type as a status type. He was like the medieval cleric, most of whose energies were devoted to separating himself from the mob—which in modern times, in Revel's phrase, goes under the name of the middle class.

Did he want to analyze the world systematically? Did he want to add to the store of human knowledge? He not only didn't want to, he belittled the notion, quoting Rosa Luxemburg's statement that the "pot-bellied academics" and their interminable monographs and lectures, their intellectual nerve gas, were sophisticated extensions of police repression. Did he even want to change the world? Not particularly; it was much more elegant to back exotic, impossible causes such as the Black Panthers'. Moral indignation was the main thing; that, and a certain pattern of consumption. In fact, by the 1960's it was no longer necessary to produce literature, scholarship, or art—or even to be involved in such matters, except as a consumer—in order to qualify as an intellectual. It was only necessary to live *la vie intellectuelle.* A little brown bread in the bread box, a lapsed pledge card to CORE, a stereo and a record rack full of Coltrane and all the Beatles albums from *Revolver* on, white walls, a huge *Dracaena marginata* plant, which is there because all the furniture is so clean-lined and spare that without this piece of frondose tropical Victoriana the room looks empty, a stack of unread *New York Review of Books* rising up in a surly mound of subscription guilt, the conviction that America is materialistic, repressive, bloated, and deadened by its Silent Majority, which resides in the heartland, three grocery boxes full of pop bottles wedged in behind the refrigerator and destined (one of these days) for the Recycling Center, a small, uncomfortable European car—that pretty well got the job done. By the late 1960's it seemed as if American intellectuals had at last . . . Caught Up. There were riots on the campuses and in the slums. The war in Vietnam had developed into a full-sized hell. War! Revolution! Imperialism! Poverty! I can still remember the ghastly delight with which literary people in New York embraced the Four Horsemen. The dark night was about to descend. All agreed on that; but there were certain ugly, troublesome facts that the native intellectuals, unlike their European mentors, had a hard time ignoring.

By 1967 Lyndon Johnson may have been the very generalissimo of American imperialism in Southeast Asia—but back here in the U.S. the citizens were enjoying freedom of expression and freedom of dissent to a rather astonishing degree. For example, the only major Western country that allowed public showings of *MacBird*—a play that had Lyndon Johnson murdering John F. Kennedy in order to become President—was the United States (Lyndon Johnson, President). The citizens of this fascist bastion, the United States, unaccountably had, and exercised, the most extraordinary political freedom and civil rights in all history. In fact, the government, under the same Johnson, had begun the novel experiment of sending organizers into the slums—in the Community Action phase of the poverty program—to mobilize minority groups to rise up against the government and demand a bigger slice of the pie. (They obliged.) Colored peoples were much farther along the road to equality—whether in the area of rights, jobs, income, or social acceptance—in the United States than were the North Africans, Portuguese, Senegalese, Pakistanis, and Jamaicans of Europe. In 1966 England congratulated herself over the appointment of her first colored policeman (a Pakistani in Coventry). Meanwhile, young people in the U.S.—in the form of the Psychedelic or Flower Generation—were helping themselves to wild times that were the envy of children all over the world.

In short, freedom was in the air like a flock of birds. Just how fascist could it be? This problem led to perhaps the greatest Adjectival Catch Up of all times: Herbert Marcuse's doctrine of "repressive tolerance." Other countries had real repression? Well, we had the obverse, repressive tolerance. This was an insidious system through which the government granted meaningless personal freedoms in order to narcotize the pain of class repression, which only socialism could cure. Beautiful! Well-nigh flawless!

Yet even at the moment of such exquisite refinements—things have a way of going wrong. Another troublesome fact has cropped up, gravely complicating the longtime dream of socialism. That troublesome fact may be best summed up in a name: Solzhenitsyn.

5. *Blaming the messenger*

With the Hungarian uprising of 1956 and the invasion of Czechoslovakia in 1968 it had become clear to Mannerist Marxists such as Sartre that the Soviet Union was now an embarrassment. The fault, however, as *tout le monde* knew, was not with socialism but with Stalinism. Stalin was a madman and had taken socialism on a wrong turn. (Mistakes happen.) Solzhenitsyn began speaking out as a dissident inside the Soviet Union in 1967. His complaints, his revelations, his struggles with Soviet authorities—they merely underscored just how wrong the Stalinist turn had been.

The publication of *The Gulag Archipelago* in 1973, however, was a wholly unexpected blow. No one was ready for the obscene horror and grotesque scale of what Solzhenitsyn called "Our Sewage Disposal System"—in which *tens of millions* were shipped in boxcars to concentration camps all over the country, in which tens of millions died, in which entire races and national groups were liquidated, insofar as they had existed in the Soviet Union. Moreover, said Solzhenitsyn, the system had not begun with Stalin but with Lenin, who had immediately exterminated non-Bolshevik opponents of the old regime and especially the student factions. It was impossible any longer to distinguish the Communist liquidation apparatus from the Nazi.

Yet Solzhenitsyn went still further. He said that not only Stalinism, not only Leninism, not only Communism—but socialism itself led to the concentration camps; and not only socialism, but Marxism; and not only Marxism but any ideology that sought to reorganize morality on an *a priori* basis. Sadder still, it was impossible to say that Soviet socialism was not "real socialism." On the contrary—it was socialism done by experts!

Intellectuals in Europe and America were willing to forgive Solzhenitsyn a great deal. After all, he had been born and raised in the Soviet Union as a Marxist, he had fought in combat for his country, he was a great novelist, he had been in the camps for eight years, he had suffered. But for his insistence that the *isms* themselves led to the death camps—for this he was not likely to be forgiven soon. And in fact the campaign of antisepsis began soon after he was expelled from the Soviet Union in 1974. ("He suffered *too* much—he's crazy." "He's a Christian zealot with a Christ complex." "He's an agrarian reactionary." "He's an egotist and a publicity junkie.")

Solzhenitsyn's tour of the United States in 1975 was like an enormous funeral procession that no one wanted to see. The White House wanted no part of him. *The New York Times* sought to bury his two major speeches, and only the moral pressure of a lone *Times* writer, Hilton Kramer, brought them any appreciable coverage at all. The major television networks declined to run the Solzhenitsyn interview that created such a stir in England earlier this year (it ran on some of the educational channels).

And the literary world in general ignored him completely. In the huge unseen coffin that Solzhenitsyn towed behind him were not only the souls of the *zeks* who died in the Archipelago. No, the heartless bastard had also chucked in one of the last great visions: the intellectual as the Stainless Steel Socialist glistening against the bone heap of capitalism in its final, brutal, fascist phase. There was a bone heap, all right, and it was grisly beyond belief, but socialism had created it.

·   ·   ·

IN 1974, IN ONE OF HIS LAST SPEECHES, THE LATE LIONEL Trilling, who was probably the most prestigious literary critic in the country and had been a professor of English at Columbia for thirty-five years, made what falls under the heading of "a modest proposal." He suggested that the liberal-arts curriculum in the universities be abandoned for one generation.

His argument ran as follows: Children come to the university today, and they register, and they get the student-activity card and the map of the campus and the university health booklet, and just about as automatically they get a packet of cultural and political attitudes. That these attitudes are negative or cynical didn't seem to be what worried Trilling. It was more that they are dispensed and accepted with such an air of conformity and inevitability. The student emerges from the university with a set of ready-mades, intact, untouched by direct experience. What was the solution? Well—why not turn off the packaging apparatus for a while? In time there might develop a generation of intelligent people who had experienced American life directly and "earned" their opinions.

Whether his proposal was serious or not, I couldn't say. But somehow he made me think once more of the Lost Lad of the Great Plains, the Candide in Reverse,

Who asked how old you had to be
Before the O'Hare curse
Coldcocked you like the freight train
Of history—
Tell me, are you willing,
Lost Lad, to pick yourself some
Intelligent lost coed Cunégonde
And head out shank-to-flank in Trilling's
Curriculum?

Will you hector tout le monde?
Will you sermonize
On how perceiving
Is believing
The heresy of your own eyes?

chapter VI

The Me Decade and the Third Great Awakening

1. Me and my hemorrhoids

THE TRAINER SAID, "TAKE YOUR FINGER OFF THE REPRESS button." Everybody was supposed to let go, let all the vile stuff come up and gush out. They even provided vomit bags, like the ones on a 747, in case you literally let it *gush out!* Then the trainer told everybody to think of "the one thing you would most like to eliminate from your life." And so what does our girl blurt over the microphone?

"Hemorrhoids!"

Just so!

That was how she ended up in her present state . . . stretched out on the wall-to-wall carpet of a banquet hall in the Ambassador Hotel in Los Angeles with her eyes closed and her face pressed into the stubble of the carpet, which is a thick commercial weave and feels like clothesbrush bristles against her face and smells a bit *high* from cleaning solvent. That was how she ended up lying here concentrating on her hemorrhoids.

Eyes shut! deep in her own space! her hemorrhoids! the grisly peanut—

Many others are stretched out on the carpet all around her; some 249 other souls, in fact. They're all strewn across the floor of the banquet hall with their eyes closed, just as she is. But, Christ, the others are concentrating on things that sound serious and deep when you talk about them. And how they had talked about them! They had all marched right up to the microphone and "shared," as the trainer called it. What did they want to eliminate from their lives? Why, they took their fingers right off the old repress button and told the whole room. My husband! my wife! my homosexuality! my inability to communicate, my self-hatred, self-destructiveness, craven fears, puling weaknesses, primordial horrors, premature ejaculation, impotence, frigidity, rigidity, subservience, laziness, alcoholism, major vices, minor vices, grim habits, twisted psyches, tortured souls—and then it had been her turn, and she had said, "Hemorrhoids."

You can imagine what that sounded like. That broke the place up. The trainer looked like a cocky little bastard up there on the podium, with his deep tan, white tennis shirt, and peach-colored sweater, a dynamite color combination, all very casual and spontaneous—after about two hours of trying on different outfits in front of a mirror, *that* kind of casual and spontaneous, if her guess was right. And yet she found him attractive. *Commanding* was the word. He probably wondered if she was playing the wiseacre, with her "hemorrhoids," but he rolled with it. Maybe she *was* being playful. Just looking at him made her feel mischievous. In any event, *hemorrhoids* was what had bubbled up into her brain.

Then the trainer had told them to stack their folding chairs in the back of the banquet hall and lie down on the floor and close their eyes and get deep into their own spaces and concentrate on that one item they wanted to get rid of most—and really feel it and let the feeling gush out.

So now she's lying here concentrating on her hemorrhoids. The strange thing is . . . it's no joke after all! She begins to feel her hemorrhoids in all their morbid presence. She can actually *feel* them. The sieges always began with her having the sensation that a peanut was caught in her anal sphincter. That meant a section of swollen varicose vein had pushed its way out of her intestines and was actually coming out of her bottom. It was as hard as a peanut and felt bigger and grislier than a peanut. Well—for God's sake!—in her daily life, even at work, *especially* at work, and she works for a movie distributor, her whole picture of herself was of her . . . *seductive physical presence*. She was not the most successful businesswoman in Los Angeles, but she was certainly successful enough, and quite in addition to that, she was . . . *the main sexual presence in the office*. When she walked into the office each morning, everyone, women as well as men, checked her out. She *knew* that. She could feel her sexual presence go through the place like an invisible chemical, like a hormone, a scent, a universal solvent.

The most beautiful moments came when she was in her office or in a conference room or at Mr. Chow's taking a meeting—nobody "had" meetings any more, they "took" them—with two or three men, men she had never met before or barely knew. The overt subject was, inevitably, eternally, "the deal." She always said there should be only one credit line up on the screen for any movie: "Deal by . . ." But the meeting would also have a subplot. The overt plot would be "The Deal." The subplot would be "The Men Get Turned On by Me." Pretty soon, even though the conversation had not strayed overtly from "the deal," the men would be swaying in unison like dune grass at the beach. And she was the wind, of course. And then one of the men would say something and smile and at the same time reach over and touch her . . . on top of the hand or on the side of the arm . . . as if it meant nothing . . . as if it were just a gesture for emphasis . . . *but, in fact, a man is usually deathly afraid of reaching out and touching a woman he doesn't know* . . . and she knew it meant she had hypnotized him sexually . . .

Well—for God's sake!—at just that sublime moment, likely as not, the goddamn peanut would be popping out of her tail! As she smiled sublimely at her conquest, she also had to sit in her chair lopsided, with one cheek of her buttocks higher than the other, as if she were about to crepitate, because it hurt to sit squarely on the peanut. If for any reason she had to stand up at that point and walk, she would have to walk as if her hip joints were rusted out, as if she were sixty-five years old, because a normal stride pressed the peanut, and the pain would start up, and the bleeding, too, very likely. Or if she couldn't get up and had to sit there for a while and keep her smile and her hot hormonal squinted eyes pinned on the men before her, the peanut would start itching or burning, and she would start double-tracking, as if her mind were a tape deck with two channels going at once. In one she's the sexual princess, the Circe, taking a meeting and clouding men's minds . . . and in the other she's a poor bitch who wants nothing more in this world than to go down the corridor to the ladies' room and get some Kleenex and some Vaseline and push the peanut back up into her intestines with her finger.

And even if she's able to get away and do that, she will spend the rest of that day and the next, and the next, with a *deep worry* in the back of her brain, the sort of worry that always stays on the edge of your consciousness, no matter how hard you think of something else. She will be wondering at all times what the next bowel movement will be like, how solid and compact the bolus will be, trying to think back and remember if she's had any milk, cream, chocolate, or any other binding substance in the last twenty-four hours, or any nuts or fibrous vegetables like broccoli. Is she really *in for it* this time—

The Sexual Princess! On the outside she has on her fireproof grin and her Fiorio scarf, as if to say she lives in a world of

Sevilles and 450SL's and dinner last night at Dominick's, a movie business restaurant on Beverly Boulevard that's so exclusive, Dominick keeps his neon sign *(Dominick's)* turned off at night to make the wimps think it's closed, but *she* (Hi, Dominick!) can get a table—while inside her it's all the battle between the bolus and the peanut—

—and is it too late to leave the office and go get some mineral oil and let some of that vile glop roll down her gullet or get a refill on the softener tablets or eat some prunes or drink some coffee or do something else to avoid one of those horrible hard-clay boluses that will come grinding out of her, crushing the peanut and starting not only the bleeding but . . . *the pain!* . . . a horrible humiliating pain that feels like she's getting a paper cut in her anus, like the pain you feel when the edge of a piece of bond paper slices your finger, plus a horrible hellish purple bloody varicose pressure, but lasting not for an instant, like a paper cut, but for an eternity, prolonged until the tears are rolling down her face as she sits in the cubicle, and she wants to cry out, to scream until it's over, to make the screams of fear, fury, and humiliation obliterate the pain. But someone would hear! No doubt they'd come bursting right into the ladies' room to save her! and feed and water their morbid curiosities! And what could she possibly say? And so she had simply held that feeling in all these years, with her eyes on fire and her entire pelvic saddle a great purple tub of pain. She had repressed the whole squalid horror of it— *the searing peanut*—until now. The trainer had said, "Take your finger off the repress button!" Let it gush up and pour out!

And now, as she lies here on the floor of the banquet hall of the Ambassador Hotel with 249 other souls, she knows exactly what he meant. She can feel it *all,* all of the pain, and on top of the pain all the humiliation, and for the first time in her life she has permission from the Management, from herself and everyone around her, to let the feeling gush forth. So she starts moaning.

"Oooooooooooooooooooooooooohhhhhhhhhhhhhhhhhhhhh!"

And when she starts moaning, the most incredible and exhilarating thing begins to happen. A wave of moans spreads through the people lying around her, as if her energy were radiating out like a radar pulse.

"Ooooooooooooooooooooooohhhhhhhhh!"

So she lets her moan rise into a keening sound.

"Ooooooooooooooooooohhhhhhhhhhheeeeeeeeeeeeeeeeeeeeeeeeee!"

And when she begins to keen, the souls near her begin keening, even while the moans are still spreading to the prostrate folks farther from her, on the edges of the room.

"Eeeeeeeeeeeeeeoooooooohhhhhhhhhhheeeeeeeeeeeeeeeeooooooooh!"

So she lets her keening sound rise up into a real scream.

"Eeeeeeeeeeeeeeeeeeaiaiaiaiaiaiaiaiaiaiaiaiaiaiaiaiai!"

And this rolls out in a wave, too, first through those near her, and then toward the far edges.

"Aiaiaiaiaiaiaiaiaiaiaiaiaieeeeeeeeeeeeeeeeeeeeohhhhhhhhhheeeeeaiaiai!"

And so she turns it all the way up, into a scream such as she has never allowed herself in her entire life.

"AiaiaiaiaiaiaiaiaaaAAAAAAAAAAAAAAAARRRRRRGGGGGGGHHHHHH!"

And her full scream spreads from soul to soul, over the top of the keens and fading moans—

"AAAAAAARRRRRGGGGHHHaiaiaiaiaiaieeeeeeeeeeoooooohhheeeeeeeaiaiaiaiaaaAAAAAAAAAARRRRRRRGGGGGGHHHHHHHHHHHHHH!"

—until at last the entire room is consumed in her scream, as if there are no longer 250 separate souls but one noösphere of souls united in some incorporeal way by her scream—

"AAAAAAAAARRRRRRRGGGGGGGHHHHHHHH!"

—which is not simply *her* scream any longer . . . but the world's! Each soul is concentrated on its own burning item—my husband! my wife! my homosexuality! my inability to communicate, my self-hatred, self-destruction, craven fears, puling weaknesses, primordial horrors, premature ejaculation, impotence, frigidity, rigidity, subservience, laziness, alcoholism, major vices, minor vices, grim habits, twisted psyches, tortured souls—and yet each unique item has been raised to a cosmic level and united with every other until there is but one piercing moment of release and liberation at last!—a whole world of anguish set free by—

My hemorrhoids.

"Me and My Hemorrhoids Star at the Ambassador" ... during a three-day Erhard Seminars Training (est) course in the banquet hall. The truly odd part, however, is yet to come. In her experience lies the explanation of certain grand puzzles of the 1970's, a period that will come to be known as the Me Decade.

2. The holy roll

In 1972 a farsighted caricaturist did this drawing of Teddy Kennedy, entitled "President Kennedy campaigning for reelection in 1980 ... courting the so-called Awakened vote." The picture shows Kennedy ostentatiously wearing not only a crucifix but also (if one looks just above the cross) a pendant of the Bleeding Heart of Jesus. The crucifix is the symbol of Christianity in general, but the Bleeding Heart is the symbol of some of Christianity's most ecstatic, non-rational, holy-rolling cults. I should point out that the artist's prediction lacked certain refinements. For one thing, Kennedy may be campaigning to be President in 1980, but he is not terribly likely to be the incumbent. For another, the odd spectacle of politicians using ecstatic, non-rational, holy-rolling religion in Presidential campaigning was to appear first not in 1980 but in 1976.

The two most popular new figures in the 1976 campaign, Jimmy Carter and Jerry Brown, are men who rose up from state politics ... absolutely aglow with mystical religious streaks. Carter turned out to be an evangelical Baptist who had recently been "born again" and "saved," who had "accepted Jesus Christ as my personal Savior"—i.e., he was of the Missionary lectern-

President Kennedy campaigning for reelection in 1980 . . . courting the so-called Awakened vote

pounding Amen ten-finger C-major chord Sister-Martha-at-the-Yamaha-keyboard loblolly piney-woods Baptist faith in which the members of the congregation stand up and "give witness" and "share it, Brother" and "share it, Sister" and "praise God!" during the service.* Jerry Brown turned out to be the Zen Jesuit, a former Jesuit seminarian who went about like a hairshirt Catholic monk, but one who happened to believe also in the Gautama Buddha, and who got off koans in an offhand but confident manner, even on political issues, as to how it is not the right answer that matters but the right question, and so forth.

Newspaper columnists and news-magazine writers continually referred to the two men's "enigmatic appeal." Which is to say, they couldn't explain it. Nevertheless, they tried. They theorized that the war in Vietnam, Watergate, the FBI and CIA scandals had left the electorate shell-shocked and disillusioned and that in their despair the citizens were groping no longer for specific remedies but for sheer faith, something, anything (even holy rolling), to believe in. This was in keeping with the current fashion of interpreting all new political phenomena in terms of recent disasters, frustration, protest, the decline of civilization . . . the Grim Slide. But when *The New York Times* and CBS employed a polling organization to try to find out just what great gusher of "frustration" and "protest" Carter had hit, the results were baffling. A Harvard political scientist, William Schneider, con-

---

*Carter is not, however, a member of the most down-home and ecstatic of the Baptist sects, which is a back-country branch known as the Primitive Baptist Church. In the Primitive Baptist churches men and women sit on different sides of the room, no musical instruments are allowed, and there is a good deal of foot-washing and other rituals drawn from passages in the Bible. The Progressive Primitives, another group, differ from the Primitives chiefly in that they allow a piano or organ in the church. The Missionary Baptists, Carter's branch, are a step up socially (not necessarily divinely) but would not be a safe bet for an ambitious member of an in-town country club. The In-town Baptists, found in communities of 25,000 or more, are too respectable, socially, to be called ecstatic and succeed in being almost as tame as the Episcopalians, Presbyterians, and Methodists.

cluded for the Los Angeles *Times* that "the Carter protest" was a
new kind of protest, "a protest of good feelings." That was a new
kind, sure enough: a protest that wasn't a protest.

In fact, both Carter and Brown had stumbled upon a fabulous
terrain for which there are no words in current political language. A couple of politicians had finally wandered into the Me
Decade.

3. Him?—the new man?

The saga of the Me Decade begins with one of those facts that are
so big and so obvious (like the Big Dipper) no one ever comments
on them anymore. Namely: the thirty-year boom. Wartime
spending in the United States in the 1940's touched off a boom
that has continued for more than thirty years. It has pumped
money into every class level of the population on a scale without
parallel in any country in history. True, nothing has solved the
plight of those at the very bottom, the chronically unemployed of
the slums. Nevertheless, in the city of Compton, California, it is
possible for a family of four at the very lowest class level, which
is known in America today as "on welfare," to draw an income
of $8,000 a year entirely from public sources. This is more than
most British newspaper columnists and Italian factory foremen
make, even allowing for differences in living costs. In America
truck drivers, mechanics, factory workers, policemen, firemen,
and garbagemen make so much money—$15,000 to $20,000 (or
more) per year is not uncommon—that the word "proletarian"
can no longer be used in this country with a straight face. So one
now says "lower middle class." One can't even call workingmen
"blue collar" any longer. They all have on collars like Joe Namath's or Johnny Bench's or Walt Frazier's. They all have on $35
superstar Qiana sport shirts with elephant collars and 1940's Air-
brush Wallpaper Flowers Buncha Grapes & Seashell designs all
over them.

Well, my God, the old utopian socialists of the nineteenth cen-

tury—such as Saint-Simon, Owen, Fourier, and Marx—*lived* for
the day of the liberated workingman. They foresaw a day when
industrialism (Saint-Simon coined the word) would give the
common man the things he needed in order to realize his potential as a human being: surplus (discretionary) income, political
freedom, free time (leisure), and freedom from grinding
drudgery. Some of them, notably Owen and Fourier, thought all
this might come to pass first in the United States. So they set up
communes here: Owen's New Harmony commune in Indiana
and thirty-four Fourier-style "phalanx" settlements—socialist
communes, because the new freedom was supposed to be possible only under socialism. The old boys never dreamed that it
would come to pass instead as the result of a Go-Getter Bourgeois business boom such as began in the U.S. in the 1940's. Nor
would they have liked it if they had seen it. For one thing, the
homo novus, the new man, the liberated man, the first common
man in the history of the world with the much-dreamed-of combination of money, freedom, and free time—this American
workingman—didn't *look* right. The Joe Namath–Johnny
Bench–Walt Frazier superstar Qiana wallpaper sports shirts, for
a start.

He didn't look right . . . and he wouldn't . . . *do right!* I can remember what brave plans visionary architects at Yale and Harvard still had for *the common man* in the early 1950's. (They
actually used the term "the common man.") They had brought
the utopian socialist dream forward into the twentieth century.
They had things figured out for the workingman down to truly
minute details, such as lamp switches. The new liberated workingman would live as the Cultivated Ascetic. He would be mod-
eled on the B.A.-degree Greenwich Village bohemian of the late
1940's—dark wool Hudson Bay shirts, tweed jackets, flannel
trousers, briarwood pipes, good books, sandals and simplicity—
except that he would live in a Worker Housing project. All Yale
and Harvard architects worshipped Bauhaus principles and had
the Bauhaus vision of Worker Housing. The Bauhaus movement

absolutely hypnotized American architects, once its leaders, such as Walter Gropius and Ludwig Mies van der Rohe, came to the United States from Germany in the 1930's. Worker Housing in America would have pure beige rooms, stripped, freed, purged of all moldings, cornices, and overhangs—which Gropius regarded as symbolic "crowns" and therefore loathsome. Worker Housing would be liberated from all wallpaper, "drapes," Wilton rugs with flowers on them, lamps with fringed shades and bases that looked like vases or Greek columns. It would be cleansed of all doilies, knickknacks, mantelpieces, headboards, and radiator covers. Radiator coils would be left bare as honest, abstract sculptural objects.

But somehow the workers, incurable slobs that they were, avoided Worker Housing, better known as "the projects," as if it had a smell. They were heading out instead to the suburbs—the *suburbs!*—to places like Islip, Long Island, and the San Fernando Valley of Los Angeles—and buying houses with clapboard siding and pitched roofs and shingles and gaslight-style front-porch lamps and mailboxes set up on top of lengths of stiffened chain that seemed to defy gravity, and all sorts of other unbelievably cute or antiquey touches, and they loaded these houses with "drapes" such as baffled all description and wall-to-wall carpet you could lose a shoe in, and they put barbecue pits and fish ponds with concrete cherubs urinating into them on the lawn out back, and they parked twenty-five-foot-long cars out front and Evinrude cruisers up on tow trailers in the carport just beyond the breezeway.*

---

*Ignored or else held in contempt by working people, Bauhaus design eventually triumphed as a symbol of wealth and privilege, attuned chiefly to the tastes of businessmen's wives. For example, Mies's most famous piece of furniture design, the Barcelona chair, now sells for $1,680 and is available only through one's decorator. The high price is due in no small part to the chair's Worker Housing Honest Materials: stainless steel and leather. No chromed iron is allowed, and customers are refused if they want to have the chair upholstered in material of their own choice. Only leather is allowed, and only six shades of that: Seagram's Building Lobby

By the 1960's the common man was also getting quite interested in this business of "realizing his potential as a human being." But once again he crossed everybody up! Once more he took his money and ran—determined to do-it-himself!

4. Plugging in

In 1971 I made a lecture tour of Italy, talking (at the request of my Italian hosts) about "contemporary American life." Everywhere I went, from Turin to Palermo, Italian students were interested in just one question: Was it really true that young people in America, no older than themselves, actually left home and lived communally according to their own rules and created their own dress styles and vocabulary and had free sex and took dope? They were talking, of course, about the hippie or psychedelic movement that had begun flowering about 1965. What fascinated them the most, however, was the first item on the list: that the hippies *actually left home and lived communally according to their own rules.*

To Italian students this seemed positively amazing. Several of the students I met lived wild enough lives during daylight hours. They were in radical organizations and had fought pitched battles with police, *on the barricades,* as it were. But by 8:30 p.m. they were back home, obediently washing their hands before dinner with Mom and Dad and Buddy and Sis and the Maiden Aunt. When they left home for good, it was likely to be via the only admissible ticket: marriage. Unmarried sons of thirty-eight and thirty-nine would still be sitting around the same old table, morosely munching the gnocchi.

Meanwhile, ordinary people in America were breaking off from conventional society, from family, neighborhood, and com-

Relates to Europe

Palomino, Monsanto Chemical Company Lobby Antelope, Arco Towers Pecan, Trans-America Building Ebony, Bank of America Building Walnut, and Architectural Digest Mink.

munity, and creating worlds of their own. This had no parallel in history, certainly considering the scale of it. The hippies were merely the most flamboyant example. The New Left students of the late 1960's were another. The New Lefters lived in communes much like the hippies' but with a slightly different emphasis. Dope, sex, nudity, costumes, and vocabulary became symbols of defiance of bourgeois life. The costumery tended to be semi-military: non-com officers' shirts, combat boots, commando berets—worn in combination with blue jeans or a turtleneck jersey, however, to show that one wasn't a uniform freak.

That people so young could go off on their own, without taking jobs, and live a life completely of their own design—to Europeans it was astounding. That ordinary factory workers could go off to the suburbs and buy homes and create their own dream houses—this, too, was astounding. And yet the new life of old people in America in the 1960's was still more astounding. Throughout European history and in the United States up to the Second World War, old age was a time when you had to cling to your children or other kinfolk, and to their sufferance and mercy, if any. The Old Folks at Home happily mingling in the old manse with the generations that followed? The little ones learning at Grandpa's and Grandma's bony knees? These are largely the myths of nostalgia. The beloved old folks were often exiled to the attic or the outbuildings, and the servants brought them their meals. They were not considered decorative in the dining room or the parlor.

In the 1960's, old people in America began doing something that was more extraordinary than it ever seemed at the time. They cut through the whole dreary humiliation of old age by heading off to "retirement villages" and "leisure developments"—which quickly became Old Folks communes. Some of the old parties managed to take this to a somewhat psychedelic extreme. For example, the trailer caravaners. The caravaners were (and are) mainly retired couples who started off their Golden Years by doing the usual thing. They went to their children, Buddy and Sis, and gingerly suggested that now that Dad had retired, he and Mom might move in with one of them. They get the old "Uhh . . . sure"—plus a death-ray look. So the two old crocks depart and go out and buy what is the only form of pre-fabricated housing that has ever caught on in America: the house trailer, or mobile home. Usually the old pair would try to make the trailer look like a real house. They'd park it on a plot in a trailer park and put it up on blocks and put some latticework around the bottom to hide the axles and the wheel housings and put little awnings above the windows and a big one out over the door to create the impression of a breezeway. By and by, however, they would discover that there were people their age who actually moved off dead center with these things and went out into the world and *rolled.* At this point they would join a trailer caravan. And when the trailer caravans got rolling, you had a chance to see some of the most amazing sights of the modern American landscape . . . such as thirty, forty, fifty Airstream trailers, the ones that are silver and have rounded corners and ends and look like silver bullets . . . thirty, forty, fifty of these silver bullets in a line, in a caravan, hauling down the highway in the late after-noon with the sun at a low angle and exploding off the silver sur-faces of the Airstreams until the whole convoy looks like some gigantic and improbable string of jewelry, each jewel ablaze with a highlight, rolling over the face of the earth—the million-volt, billion-horsepower bijoux of America!

The caravaners might start off taking the ordinary tourist routes of the West, but they would soon get a taste for adventure and head for the badlands, through the glacier forests of the Northwest and down through western Mexico, not fat green chile relleno red jacaranda blossom mariachi band caballero som-brero Tourist Mexico but *western* Mexico, where the terrain is all skulls and bones and junk frito and hardcheese mestizos hun-kered down at the crossroads, glowering, and cows and armadil-los by the side of the road on their backs with their bellies bloated and all four feet up in the air. The caravaners would get deeper and deeper into a life of sheer *trailering*. They would become experts at this twentieth-century nomad life. They would begin to look back on Buddy & Sis as sad conventional sorts whom they had left behind, poor turkeys who knew nothing of the initiations and rites of passage of trailering.

The mighty million-volt rites! Every now and then the caravan would have to seek out a trailer camp for a rest in the rush across the face of Western America, and in these camps you'd have to plug a power line from your trailer into the utility poles the camps provide, so as to be able to use the appliances in the trailer when your car engine wasn't generating electricity. In some of the older camps these poles were tricky to use. If you didn't plug your line in in just the right manner, with the right prong up and the right one down, you stood to get a hell of a shock, a feedback of what felt like about two thousand volts. So about dusk you might see the veterans sitting outside their trailers in aluminum-and-vinyl folding chairs, pretending to be just chewing the fat at sunset but in fact nudging one another and keeping everyone on the alert for what is about to happen when the rookie—the rheumy-eyed, gray-haired old Dad who, with Mom, has just joined the caravan—plugs into the malicious Troll Pole for the first time.

Old Dad tries to plug in, and of course he gets it wrong, tries to put the wrong prong in on top and the wrong one on the bottom, and—*bowwwwwwww!*—he gets a thunderbolt jolt like Armageddon itself and does an inverted one-and-a-half gainer and lands on his back—and the veterans, men and women, just absolutely crack up, bawl, cry, laugh until they're turning inside out. And only after the last whoops and snorts have died down does it dawn on you that this poor wet rookie who plugged in wrong and has just done this involuntary Olympic diving maneuver and landed on his spine with his fingers smoking . . . is a gray-haired party seventy-two years old. But that's also the beauty of it! They always survive! They're initiates! hierophants of the caravan who have moved off dead center! Various deadly rheumatoid symptoms disappear, as if by magic! The Gerontoid Cowboys ride! deep into a new land and a new life they've created for themselves!

5. Lemon sessions

It was remarkable enough that ordinary folks now had enough money to take it and run off and alter the circumstances of their lives and create new roles for themselves, such as Trailer Sailor. But simultaneously still others decided to go . . . *all the way.* They plunged straight toward what has become the alchemical dream of the Me Decade.

The old alchemical dream was changing base metals into gold. The new alchemical dream is: changing one's personality—remaking, remodeling, elevating, and polishing one's very *self* . . . and observing, studying, and doting on it. (Me!) This had always been an aristocratic luxury, confined throughout most of history to the life of the courts, since only the very wealthiest classes had the free time and the surplus income to dwell upon this sweetest and vainest of pastimes. It smacked so much of vanity, in fact, that the noble folk involved in it always took care to call it quite something else.

Much of the satisfaction well-born people got from what is known historically as the "chivalric tradition" was precisely that: dwelling upon *Me* and every delicious nuance of my conduct and personality. At Versailles, Louis XIV founded a school for girls called Saint-Cyr. At the time most schools for girls were in convents. Louis had quite something else in mind, a secular school that would develop womenfolk suitable for the superior *race guerrière* that he believed himself to be creating in France. Saint-Cyr was the forerunner for what was known up until a few years ago as *the finishing school.* And what was *the finishing school?* Why, a school in which the personality was to be shaped and buffed like a piece of high-class psychological cabinetry. For centuries most of upper-class college education in France and England has been fashioned in the same manner: with an eye toward sculpting the personality as carefully as the intellectual faculties.

At Yale the students on the outside have wondered for eighty years what went on inside the fabled secret senior societies, such as Skull & Bones. On Thursday nights one would see the secret-society members walking silently and single-file, in black flannel suits, white shirts, and black knit ties with gold pins on them, toward their great Greek Revival temples, buildings whose mystery was doubled by the fact that they had no windows. What in the name of God or Mammon went on in those thirty-odd Thursday nights during the senior years of these happy few? What went on was ... *lemon sessions!*—a regularly scheduled series of the lemon sessions, just like the ones that occurred informally in girls' finishing schools.

In the girls' schools these lemon sessions tended to take place at random on nights when a dozen or so girls might end up in someone's dormitory room. One girl would become "it," and the others would rip into her personality, pulling it to pieces to analyze every defect ... her spitefulness, her awkwardness, her bad breath, embarrassing clothes, ridiculous laugh, her suck-up fawning, latent lesbianism, or whatever. The poor creature might be reduced to tears. She might blurt out the most terrible confessions, hatreds, and primordial fears. But, it was presumed, she would be the stronger for it afterward. She would be on her way toward a new personality. Likewise, in the secret societies, they held lemon sessions for boys. Is masturbation your problem? Out with the truth, you ridiculous weenie! And Thursday night after Thursday night the awful truths would out, as he who was It stood up before them and answered the most horrible questions. Yes! I do it! I whack whack whack it! I'm *afraid* of women! I'm afraid of *you!* And I get my shirts at Rosenberg's instead of Press! (Oh, you dreary turkey, you wet smack, you little shit!) ... But out of the fire and the heap of ashes would come a better man, a brother, of good blood and good bone, for the American *race guerrière*. And what was more ... they loved it. No matter how dreary the soap opera, the star was *Me*.

By the mid-1960's this service, this luxury, had become available for one and all, i.e., the middle classes. Lemon Session Central was the Esalen Institute, a lodge perched on a cliff overlooking the Pacific in Big Sur, California. Esalen's specialty was lube jobs for the personality. Businessmen, businesswomen, housewives—anyone who could afford it, and by now many could—paid $220 a week to come to Esalen to learn about themselves and loosen themselves up and wiggle their fannies a bit, in keeping with methods developed by William C. Schutz and Frederick Perls. Fritz Perls, as he was known, was a remarkable figure, a psychologist who had a gray beard and went about in a blue terry-cloth jumpsuit and looked like a great blue grizzled father bear. His lemon sessions sprang not out of the Manly Virtues & Cold Showers Protestant Prep-School tradition of Yale but out of psychoanalysis. His sessions were a variety of the "marathon encounter."* He put the various candidates for personality change in groups, and they stayed together in close quarters day after day. They were encouraged to bare their own souls and to strip away one another's defensive façade. Everyone was to face his own emotions squarely for the first time.

Encounter sessions, particularly of the Schutz variety, were often wild events. Such aggression! such sobs! tears! moans, hysteria, vile recriminations, shocking revelations, such explosions of hostility between husbands and wives, such mudballs of profanity from previously mousy mommies and workadaddies, such red-mad attacks! Only physical assault was prohibited. The encounter session became a standard approach in many other movements, such as Scientology, Arica, the Mel Lyman move-

---

*The real "marathons," in which the group stayed in the same room for twenty-four hours or longer, were developed by George R. Bach and Frederick Stoller of Los Angeles.

ment, Synanon, Daytop Village, and Primal Scream. Synanon had started out as a drug-rehabilitation program, but by the late 1960's the organization was recruiting "lay members," a lay member being someone who had never been addicted to heroin . . . but was ready for the lemon-session life.

Outsiders, hearing of these sessions, wondered what on earth their appeal was. Yet the appeal was simple enough. It is summed up in the notion: "Let's talk about *Me.*" No matter whether you managed to renovate your personality through encounter sessions or not, you had finally focused your attention and your energies on the most fascinating subject on earth: *Me.* Not only that, you also put *Me* onstage before a live audience. The popular est movement has managed to do that with great refinement. Just imagine . . . *Me and My Hemorrhoids* . . . moving an entire hall to the most profound outpouring of emotion! Just imagine . . . *my life* becoming a drama with universal significance . . . analyzed, like Hamlet's, for what it signifies for the rest of mankind . . .

The encounter session—although it was not called that—was also a staple practice in psychedelic communes and, for that matter, in New Left communes. In fact, the analysis of the self, and of one another, was unceasing. But in these groups and at Esalen and in movements such as Arica there were two common assumptions that distinguished them from the aristocratic lemon sessions and personality *finishings* of yore. The first was: I, with the help of my brothers and sisters, must strip away all the shams and excess baggage of society and my upbringing in order to find the Real Me. Scientology uses the word "clear" to identify the state that one must strive for. But just what is that state? And what will the Real Me be like? It is at this point that the new movements tend to take on a religious or spiritual atmosphere. In one form or another they arrive at an axiom first propounded by the Gnostic Christians some eighteen hundred years ago: namely, that at the apex of every human soul there exists a spark of the light of God. In most mortals that spark is "asleep" (the Gnostics' word), all but smothered by the façades and general falseness of society. But those souls who are clear can find that spark within themselves and unite their souls with God's. And with that conviction comes the second assumption: there is an *other order* that actually reigns supreme in the world. Like the light of God itself, this *other order* is invisible to most mortals. But he who has dug himself out from under the junk heap of civilization can discover it.

And with that . . . the Me movements were about to turn *righteous*.

6. Young faith, aging groupies

By the early 1970's so many of the Me movements had reached this Gnostic religious stage, they now amounted to a new religious wave. Synanon, Arica, and the Scientology movement had become religions. The much-publicized psychedelic or hippie communes of the 1960's, although no longer big items in the press, were spreading widely and becoming more and more frankly religious. The huge Steve Gaskin commune in the Tennessee scrublands was a prime example. A *New York Times* survey concluded that there were at least two thousand communes in the United States by 1970, barely five years after the idea first caught on in California. Both the Esalen-style and Primal Therapy or Primal Scream encounter movements were becoming progressively less psychoanalytical and more mystical in their approach. The Oriental "meditation" religions—which had existed in the United States mainly in the form of rather intellectual and bohemian zen and yoga circles—experienced a spectacular boom. Groups such as the Hare Krishna, the Sufi, and the Maharaj Ji communes began to discover that they could enroll thousands of new members and (in some cases) make small fortunes in real estate to finance the expansion. Many members of the New Left communes of the 1960's began to turn up in Me movements in the 1970's, including two of the celebrated "Chicago Eight." Rennie Davis became a follower of the Maharaj Ji, Jerry

Rubin enrolled in both est and Arica. Barbara Garson—who with the help of her husband, Marvin, wrote the agitprop epic of the New Left, *MacBird*—would later observe, with considerable bitterness: "My husband, Marvin, forsook everything (me included) to find peace. For three years he wandered without shoes or money or glasses. Now he is in Israel with some glasses and possibly with some peace." And not just him, she said, but so many other New Lefters as well: "Some follow a guru, some are into primal scream, some seek a rest from the diaspora—a home in Zion." It is entirely possible that in the long run historians will regard the entire New Left experience as not so much a political as a religious episode wrapped in semi-military gear and guerrilla talk.

Meanwhile, the ESP or "psychic phenomena" movement began to grow very rapidly in the new religious atmosphere. ESP devotees had always believed that there was an *other order* that ran the universe, one that revealed itself occasionally through telepathy, *déjà vu* experiences, psychokinesis, and the like. It was but a small step from there to the assumption that all men possess a *conscious energy* paralleling the world of physical energy and that this mysterious energy can unite the universe (after the fashion of the light of God). A former astronaut, Edgar Mitchell, who has a Doctor of Science degree from M.I.T., founded the Institute of Noetic Sciences in an attempt to channel the work of all the ESP groups. "Noetic" is an adjective derived from the same root as that of "the Noösphere"—the name that Teilhard de Chardin gave his dream of a cosmic union of all souls. Even the Flying Saucer cults began to reveal their essentially religious nature at about this time. The Flying Saucer folk quite literally believed in an *other order*: it was under the command of superior beings from other planets or solar systems who had spaceships. A physician named Andrija Puharich wrote a book *(Uri)* in which he published the name of the God of the UFO's: Hoova. He said Hoova had a herald messenger named Spectra, and Hoova's and Spectra's agent on earth, the human connection, as it were, was Uri

Geller, the famous Israeli psychic and showman. Geller's powers were also of great interest to people in the ESP movement, and there were many who wished that Puharich and the UFO people would keep their hands off him.

By the early 1970's a quite surprising movement, tagged as the Jesus People, had spread throughout the country. At the outset practically all the Jesus People were young acid heads, i.e., LSD users, who had sworn off drugs (except, occasionally, in "organic form," meaning marijuana and peyote) but still wanted the ecstatic spiritualism of the psychedelic or hippie life. This they found in Fundamentalist evangelical holy-rolling Christianity of a sort that ten years before would have seemed utterly impossible to revive in America. The Jesus People, such as the Children of God, the Fresno God Squad, the Tony and Susan Alamo Christian Foundation, the Sun Myung Moon sect, lived communally and took an ecstatic or "charismatic" (literally: "God-imbued") approach to Christianity, after the manner of the Oneida, Shaker, and Mormon communes of the nineteenth century—and, for that matter, after the manner of the early Christians themselves, including the Gnostics.

There was considerable irony here. Ever since the late 1950's both the Catholic Church and the leading Protestant denominations had been aware that young people, particularly in the cities, were drifting away from the faith. At every church conference and convocation and finance committee meeting the cry went up: *We must reach the urban young people.* It became an obsession, this business of the "urban young people." The key—one and all decided—was to "modernize" and "update" Christianity. So the Catholics gave the nuns outfits that made them look like World War II Wacs. The Protestants set up "beatnik coffee houses" in the church basement for poetry reading and bongo playing. They had the preacher put on a turtleneck sweater and sing "Joe Hill" and "Frankie and Johnny" during the hootenanny at the Sunday, vespers. Both the priests and the preachers carried placards in civil rights marches, gay rights marches, women's rights marches, prisoners' rights marches, bondage lovers' rights marches, or any other marches, so long as they might appear hip to the urban young people.

In fact, all these strenuous gestures merely made the churches look like rather awkward and senile groupies of secular movements. The much-sought-after Urban Young People found the Hip Churchman to be an embarrassment, if they noticed him at all. What finally started attracting young people to Christianity was something the churches had absolutely nothing to do with: namely, the psychedelic or hippie movement. The hippies had suddenly made religion look hip. Very few people went into the hippie life with religious intentions, but many came out of it absolutely *righteous*. The sheer power of the drug LSD is not to be underestimated. It was quite easy for an LSD experience to take the form of a religious vision, particularly if one was among people already so inclined. You would come across someone you had known for years, a pal, only now he was jacked up on LSD and sitting in the middle of the street saying, "I'm in the Pudding at last! I've met the Manager!" Without knowing it, many heads were reliving the religious fervor of their grandparents or great-grandparents—the Bible-Belting lectern-pounding Amen ten-finger C-major-chord Sister-Martha-at-the-keyboard tent-meeting loblolly pineywoods share-it-brother believers of the nineteenth century. The hippies were religious and yet incontrovertibly hip at the same time.

Today it is precisely the most rational, intellectual, secularized, modernized, updated, relevant religions—all the brave, forward-looking Ethical Culture, Unitarian, and Swedenborgian movements of only yesterday—that are finished, gasping, breathing their last. What the Urban Young People want from religion is a little . . . *Hallelujah!* . . . and *talking in tongues!* . . . *Praise God!* Precisely that! In the most prestigious divinity schools today, Catholic, Presbyterian, and Episcopal, the avant-garde movement—the leading edge—is "charismatic Christianity" . . . featuring talking in tongues, ululalia, visions, holy-rolling, and other non-rational, even anti-rational, practices. Some of the most respectable old-line Protestant congregations, in the most placid suburban settings, have begun to split into the Charismatics and the Easter Christians ("All they care about is being seen in church on Easter"). The Easter Christians still usually control the main Sunday-morning service—but the Charismatics take over on Sunday evening and do the holy roll.

This curious development has breathed new life into the existing fundamentalists, theosophists, and older salvation seekers of all sorts. Ten years ago, if anyone of wealth, power, or renown had publicly "announced for Christ," people would have looked at him as if his nose had been eaten away by weevils. Today it happens regularly . . . Harold Hughes resigns from the U.S. Senate to become an evangelist . . . Jim Irwin, the astronaut, teams up with a Baptist evangelist in an organization called High Flight . . . singers like Pat Boone and Anita Bryant announce for Jesus . . . Charles Colson, the former hardballer of the Nixon Administration, announces for Jesus . . . The leading candidate for President of the United States, Jimmy Carter, announces for Jesus. O Jesus People.

7. Only one life

In 1961 a copy writer named Shirley Polykoff was working for the Foote, Cone & Belding advertising agency on the Clairol hair-dye account when she came up with the line: "If I've only one life, let me live it as a blonde!" In a single slogan she had summed up what might be described as the secular side of the Me Decade. "If I've only one life, let me live it as a ———!" (You have only to fill in the blank.)

This formula accounts for much of the popularity of the women's liberation or feminist movement. "What does a woman want?" said Freud. Perhaps there are women who want to humble men or reduce their power or achieve equality or even superiority for themselves and their sisters. But for every one such woman, there are nine who simply want to *fill in the blank* as they see fit. "If I've only one life, let me live it as . . . a free spirit!" (Instead of . . . a house slave: a cleaning woman, a cook, a nursemaid, a station wagon hacker, and an occasional household sex aid.) But even that may be overstating it, because often the unconscious desire is nothing more than: *Let's talk about Me.* The great unexpected dividend of the feminist movement has been to elevate an ordinary status—woman, housewife—to the level of drama. One's very existence as *a woman* . . . as *Me* . . . becomes something all the world analyzes, agonizes over, draws cosmic conclusions from, or, in any event, takes seriously. Every woman becomes Emma Bovary, Cousin Bette, or Nora . . . or Erica Jong or Consuelo Saah Baehr.

Among men the formula becomes: "If I've only one life, let me live it as a . . . Casanova or a Henry VIII!" (instead of a humdrum workadaddy, eternally faithful, except perhaps for a mean little skulking episode here and there, to a woman who now looks old enough to be your aunt and needs a shave or else has electrolysis lines above her upper lip, as well as atrophied calves, and is an embarrassment to be seen with when you take her on trips). The right to shuck overripe wives and take on fresh ones was once seen as the prerogative of kings only, and even then it was scandalous. In the 1950's and 1960's it began to be seen as the prerogative of the rich, the powerful, and the celebrated (Nelson Rockefeller, Henry Ford, and Show Business figures), although it retained the odor of scandal. Wife-shucking damaged Adlai Stevenson's chances of becoming President in 1952 and 1956 and Rockefeller's chances of becoming the Republican nominee in 1964 and 1968. Until the 1970's wife-shucking made it impossible for an astronaut to be chosen to go into space. Today, in the Me Decade, it becomes *normal behavior,* one of the factors that has pushed the divorce rate above 50 percent.

When Eugene McCarthy filled in the blank in 1972 and shucked his wife, it was hardly noticed. Likewise in the case of several astronauts. When Wayne Hays filled in the blank in 1976 and shucked his wife of thirty-eight years, it did not hurt his career in the slightest. Copulating with the girl in the office, however, was still regarded as scandalous. (Elizabeth Ray filled in the blank in another popular fashion: "If I've only one life, let me live it as a . . . Celebrity!" As did Arthur Bremer, who kept a diary during his stalking of Nixon and, later, George Wallace . . . with an eye toward a book contract. Which he got.) Some wiseacre has remarked, supposedly with levity, that the federal government may in time have to create reservations for women over thirty-five, to take care of the swarms of shucked wives and widows. In fact, women in precisely those categories have begun setting up communes or "extended families" to provide one another support and companionship in a world without workadaddies. ("If I've only one life, why live it as an anachronism?")

Much of what is now known as the "sexual revolution" has consisted of both women and men filling in the blank this way: "If I've only one life, let me live it as . . . a Swinger!" (Instead of a frustrated, bored monogamist.) In "swinging," a husband and wife give each other license to copulate with other people. There are no statistics on the subject that mean anything, but I do know that it pops up in conversation today in the most unexpected corners of the country. It is an odd experience to be in De Kalb, Illinois, in the very corncrib of America, and have some conventional-looking housewife (not *housewife*, damn it!) come up to you and ask: "Is there much tripling going on in New York?"

"Tripling?"

Tripling turns out to be a practice, in De Kalb, anyway, in which a husband and wife invite a third party—male or female, but more often female—over for an evening of whatever, including polymorphous perversity, even the practices written of in the one-hand magazines, such as *Hustler,* all the things involving tubes and hoses and tourniquets and cups and double-jointed sailors.

One of the satisfactions of this sort of life, quite in addition to the groin spasms, is talk: *Let's talk about Me*. Sexual adventurers are given to the most relentless and deadly serious talk ... about Me. They quickly succeed in placing themselves onstage in the sexual drama whose outlines were sketched by Freud and then elaborated by Wilhelm Reich. Men and women of all sorts, not merely swingers, are given just now to the most earnest sort of talk about the Sexual Me. A key drama of our own day is Ingmar Bergman's movie *Scenes from a Marriage*. In it we see a husband and wife who have good jobs and a well-furnished home but who are unable to "communicate"—to cite one of the signature words of the Me Decade. Then they begin to communicate, and thereupon their marriage breaks up and they start divorce proceedings. For the rest of the picture they communicate endlessly, with great candor, but the "relationship"—another signature word—remains doomed. Ironically, the lesson that people seem to draw from this movie has to do with ... "the need to communicate."

Scenes from a Marriage is one of those rare works of art, like *The Sun Also Rises,* that not only succeed in capturing a certain mental atmosphere in fictional form ... but also turn around and help radiate it throughout real life. I personally know of two instances in which couples, after years of marriage, went to see *Scenes from a Marriage* and came home convinced of the "need to communicate." The discussions began with one of the two saying, Let's try to be completely candid for once. You tell me exactly what you don't like about me, and I'll do the same for you. At this, the starting point, the whole notion is exciting. We're going to talk about *Me!* (And I can take it.) I'm going to find out what he (or she) really thinks about me! (Of course, I have my faults, but they're minor ... or else exciting.)

She says, "Go ahead. What don't you like about me?"

They're both under the Bergman spell. Nevertheless, a certain sixth sense tells him that they're on dangerous ground. So he decides to pick something that doesn't seem too terrible.

"Well," he says, "one thing that bothers me is that when we

meet people for the first time, you never know what to say. Or else you get nervous and start chattering away, and it's all so banal, it makes me look bad."

Consciously she's still telling herself, "I can take it." But what he has just said begins to seep through her brain like scalding water. What's he talking about?—makes *him* look bad? *He's saying I'm unsophisticated, a social liability and an embarrassment. All those times we've gone out, he's been ashamed of me!* (And what makes it worse—it's the sort of disease for which there's no cure!) She always knew she was awkward. His crime is: he *noticed!* He's known it, too, all along. He's had *contempt* for me.

Out loud she says, "Well, I'm afraid there's nothing I can do about that."

He detects the petulant note. "Look," he says, "you're the one who said to be candid."

She says, "I know. I *want* you to be."

He says, "Well, it's your turn."

"Well," she says, "I'll tell *you* something about when we meet people and when we go places. You never clean yourself properly—you don't know how to wipe yourself. Sometimes we're standing there talking to people, and there's . . . a smell. And I'll tell you something else: People can tell it's you."

And he's still telling *him*self, "I can take it"—but what inna namea Christ is *this?*

He says, "But you've never said anything—about anything like that."

She says, "But I *tried* to. How many times have I told you about your dirty drawers when you were taking them off at night?"

Somehow this really makes him angry . . . All those times . . . and his mind immediately fastens on Harley Thatcher and his wife, whom he has always wanted to impress . . . From underneath my $350 suits I smelled of *shit!* What infuriates him is that this is a humiliation from which there's no recovery. *How often have they sniggered about it later?—or not invited me places? Is it something people say every time my name comes up?* And all at once he is intensely annoyed with his wife, not because she never told him all these years, but simply because she *knows* about his disgrace—and she was the one who *brought him the bad news!*

From that moment on they're ready to get the skewers in. It's only a few minutes before they've begun trying to sting each other with confessions about their little affairs, their little slipping around, their little coitus on the sly—"Remember that time I told you my flight from Buffalo was canceled?"—and at that juncture the ranks of those *who can take it* become very thin indeed. So they communicate with great candor! and break up! and keep on communicating! and they find the relationship hopelessly doomed.

One couple went into group therapy. The other went to a marriage counselor. Both types of therapy are very popular forms, currently, of *Let's talk about Me.* This phase of the breakup always provides a rush of exhilaration—for what more exhilarating topic is there than . . . *Me?* Through group therapy, marriage counseling, and other forms of "psychological consultation" they can enjoy that same *Me* euphoria that the very rich have enjoyed for years in psychoanalysis. The cost of the new Me sessions is only $10 to $30 an hour, whereas psychoanalysis runs from $50 to $125. The woman's exhilaration, however, is soon complicated by the fact that she is (in the typical case) near or beyond the cutoff age of thirty-five and will have to retire to the reservation.

Well, my dear Mature Moderns . . . Ingmar never promised you a rose garden!

8. How you do it, my boys!

In September of 1969, in London, on the King's Road, in a restaurant called Alexander's, I happened to have dinner with a group of people that included a young American named Jim Haynes and an Australian named Germaine Greer. Neither name meant anything to me at the time, although I never forgot Germaine Greer. She was a thin, hard-looking woman with a tremendous curly electric hairdo and the most outrageous Naugahyde mouth I had ever heard on a woman. (I was shocked.) After a while she got bored and set fire to her hair with a match. Two waiters ran over and began beating the flames out with napkins. This made a noise like pigeons taking off in the park. Germaine Greer sat there with a sublime smile on her face, as if to say: "How you do it, my boys!"

Jim Haynes and Germaine Greer had just published the first issue of a newspaper that All London was talking about. It was called *Suck*. It was founded shortly after *Screw* in New York and was one of the progenitors of a line of sex newspapers that today are so numerous that in Los Angeles it is not uncommon to see fifteen coin-operated newspaper racks in a row on the sidewalk. One will be for the Los Angeles *Times,* a second for the *Herald Examiner,* and the other thirteen for the sex papers. *Suck* was full of pictures of gaping thighs, moist lips, stiffened giblets, glistening nodules, dirty stories, dirty poems, essays on sexual freedom, and a gossip column detailing the sexual habits of people whose names I assumed were fictitious. Then I came to an item that said, "Anyone who wants group sex in New York and likes fat girls, contact L—— R——," except that it gave her full name. She was a friend of mine.

Even while Germaine Greer's hair blazed away, the young American, Jim Haynes, went on with a discourse about the aims of *Suck*. To put it in a few words, the aim was sexual liberation and, through sexual liberation, the liberation of the spirit of man. If you were listening to this speech and had read *Suck*, or even if you hadn't, you were likely to be watching Jim Haynes's face for the beginnings of a campy grin, a smirk, a wink, a roll of the eyeballs—something to indicate that he was just having his little joke. But it soon became clear that he was one of those people who exist on a plane quite . . . Beyond Irony. Whatever it had been for him once, sex had now become a religion, and he had developed a theology in which the orgasm had become a form of spiritual ecstasy.

The same curious journey—from sexology to theology—has become a feature of *swinging* in the United States. At the Sandstone sex farm in the Santa Monica Mountains in Los Angeles people of all class levels gather for weekends in the nude. They copulate in the living room, on the lawn, out by the pool, on the tennis courts, with the same open, free, liberated spirit as dogs in the park or baboons in a tree. In conversation, however, the atmosphere is quite different. The air becomes humid with solemnity. Close your eyes, and you think you're at a nineteenth-century Wesleyan summer encampment and tent-meeting lecture series. It's the soul that gets a workout here, brethren. And yet this is not a hypocritical coverup. It is merely an example of how people in even the most secular manifestation of the Me decade—free-lance spread-'em ziggy-zig rutting—are likely to go through the usual stages . . . Let's talk about Me . . . Let's find the Real Me . . . Let's get rid of all the hypocrisies and impediments and false modesties that obscure the Real Me . . . Ah! at the apex of my soul is a spark of the Divine . . . which I perceive in the pure moment of ecstasy (which your textbooks call "the orgasm," but which I know to be heaven) . . .

This notion even has a pedigree. Many sects, such as the Left-handed Shakti and the Gnostic onanists, have construed the orgasm to be the *kairos,* the magic moment, the divine ecstasy. There is evidence that the early Mormons and the Oneida movement did likewise. In fact, the notion of some sort of divine ecstasy runs throughout the religious history of the past twenty-five hundred years. As Max Weber and Joachim Wach have illustrated in detail, every major modern religion, as well as countless long-gone minor ones, has originated not with a theology or a set of values or a social goal or even a vague hope of a life hereafter. They have all originated, instead, with a small circle of people who have shared some overwhelming ecstasy or seizure, a "vision," a "trance," a hallucination; in short, an actual neurological event, a dramatic change in metabolism, something that has seemed to light up the entire central nervous system. The Mohammedan movement (Islam) originated in hallucinations, apparently the result of fasting, meditation, and isolation in the darkness of caves, which can induce sensory deprivation. Some of the same practices were common with many types of Buddhists. The early Hindus and Zoroastrians seem to have been animated by an hallucinogenic drug known as *soma* in India and *haoma* in Persia. The origins of Christianity are replete with "visions." The early Christians used wine for ecstatic purposes, to the point where the Apostle Paul (whose conversion on the road to Damascus began with a "vision") complained that it was degenerating into sheer drunkenness at the services. These great draughts of wine survive in minute quantities in the ritual of Communion. The Bacchic orders, the Sufi, Voodooists, Shakers, and many others used feasts (the bacchanals), ecstatic dancing ("the whirling dervishes"), and other forms of frenzy to achieve the *kairos*... the *moment*... here and now!... the *feeling!*... In every case, the believers took the feeling of ecstasy to be the sensation of the light of God flooding into their souls. They felt like vessels of the Divine, of the All-in-One. Only *afterward* did they try to interpret the experience in the form of theologies, earthly reforms, moral codes, liturgies.

Nor have these been merely the strange practices of the Orient and the Middle East. Every major religious wave that has developed in America has started out the same way: with a flood of *ecstatic experiences*. The First Great Awakening, as it is known to historians, came in the 1740's and was led by preachers of the "New Light," such as Jonathan Edwards, Gilbert Tennent, and George Whitefield. They and their followers were known as "enthusiasts" and "come-outers," terms of derision that referred to the frenzied, holy-rolling, pentecostal shout tempo of their services and to their visions, trances, shrieks, and agonies, which are preserved in great Rabelaisian detail in the writings of their detractors.

The Second Great Awakening came in the period from 1825 to 1850 and took the form of a still-wilder hoedown camp-meeting revivalism, of ceremonies in which people barked, bayed, fell down in fits and swoons, rolled on the ground, talked in tongues, and even added a touch of orgy. The Second Awakening originated in western New York State, where so many evangelical movements caught fire it became known as "the Burned-over District." Many new sects, such as Oneida and the Shakers, were involved. But so were older ones, such as the evangelical Baptists. The fervor spread throughout the American frontier (and elsewhere) before the Civil War. The most famous sect of the Second Great Awakening was the Mormon movement, founded by a twenty-five-year-old, Joseph Smith, and a small group of youthful comrades. This bunch was regarded as wilder, crazier, more obscene, more of a threat, than the entire lot of hippie communes of the 1960's put together. Smith was shot to death by a lynch mob in Carthage, Illinois, in 1844, which was why the Mormons, now with Brigham Young at the helm, emigrated to Utah. A sect, incidentally, is a religion with no political power. Once the Mormons settled, built, and ruled Utah, Mormonism became a *religion* soon enough . . . and eventually wound down to the slow, firm beat of respectability . . .

We are now—in the Me Decade—seeing the upward roll (and not yet the crest, by any means) of the third great religious wave in American history, one that historians will very likely term the Third Great Awakening. Like the others it has begun in a flood of *ecstasy,* achieved through LSD and other psychedelics, orgy, dancing (the New Sufi and the Hare Krishna), meditation, and psychic frenzy (the marathon encounter). This third wave has built up from more diverse and exotic sources than the first two, from therapeutic movements as well as overtly religious movements, from hippies and students of "psi phenomena" and Flying

Saucerites as well as from charismatic Christians. But other than that, what will historians say about it?

The historian Perry Miller credited the First Great Awakening with helping to pave the way for the American Revolution through its assault on the colonies' religious establishment and, thereby, on British colonial authority generally. The sociologist Thomas F. O'Dea credited the Second Great Awakening with creating the atmosphere of Christian asceticism (known as "bleak" on the East Coast) that swept through the Midwest and the West during the nineteenth century and helped make it possible to build communities in the face of great hardship. And the Third Great Awakening? Journalists—historians have not yet tackled the subject—have shown a morbid tendency to regard the various movements in this wave as "fascist." The hippie movement was often attacked as "fascist" in the late 1960's. Over the past year a barrage of articles has attacked the est movement and the "Moonies" (followers of the Rev. Sun Myung Moon) along the same lines.

Frankly, this tells us nothing except that journalists bring the same conventional Grim Slide concepts to every subject. The word "fascism" derives from the old Roman symbol of power and authority, the *fasces,* a bundle of sticks bound together by thongs (with an ax head protruding from one end). One by one the sticks would be easy to break. Bound together they are indestructible. Fascist ideology called for binding all classes, all levels, all elements of an entire nation together into a single organization with a single will.

The various movements of the current religious wave attempt very nearly the opposite. They begin with . . . "Let's talk about Me." They begin with the most delicious look inward; with considerable narcissism, in short. When the believers bind together into religions, it is always with a sense of splitting off from the rest of society. We, the enlightened (lit by the sparks at the apexes of our souls), hereby separate ourselves from the lost souls around us. Like all religions before them, they proselytize—but always promising the opposite of nationalism: a City of Light that is above it all. There is no ecumenical spirit within this Third Great Awakening. If anything, there is a spirit of schism. The contempt the various gurus and seers have for one another is breathtaking. One has only to ask, say, Oscar Ichazo of Arica about Carlos Castaneda or Werner Erhard of est to learn that Castaneda is a fake and Erhard is a shallow sloganeer. It's exhilarating!—to watch the faithful split off from one another to seek ever more perfect and refined crucibles in which to fan the Divine spark . . . and to *talk about Me.*

Whatever the Third Great Awakening amounts to, for better or for worse, will have to do with this unprecedented post–World War II American luxury: the luxury enjoyed by so many millions of middling folk, of dwelling upon the self. At first glance, Shirley Polykoff's slogan—"If I've only one life, let me live it as a blonde!"—seems like merely another example of a superficial and irritating rhetorical trope *(antanaclasis*)* that now happens to be fashionable among advertising copy writers. But in fact the notion of "If I've only one life to live" challenges one of those assumptions of society that are so deep-rooted and ancient they have no name—they are simply lived by. In this case: man's age-old belief in serial immortality.

The husband and wife who sacrifice their own ambitions and their material assets in order to provide a "better future" for their children . . . the soldier who risks his life, or perhaps consciously

---

*This figure of speech consists of repeating a word (or words with the same root) in such a way that the second usage has a different meaning from the first. "This is WINS, 1010 on your dial—New York wants to *know,* and we *know* it" (1. know = "find out"; 2. know = "realize" or "have the knowledge") . . . "We're American Airlines, *doing* what we *do* best" (1. doing = "performing"; 2. what we do = "our job") . . . "If you think refrigerators cost *too much,* maybe you're looking at *too much* refrigerator (1. cost; 2. size or complexity). The smart money *is* on Admiral (Admiral's italics)" . . . There is also an example of the *pun* in the WINS slogan and of *epanadiplosis* in the Admiral slogan (the ABBA pattern of *refrigerator . . . too much/too much refrigerator*).

sacrifices it, in battle . . . the man who devotes his life to some struggle for "his people" that cannot possibly be won in his lifetime . . . people (or most of them) who buy life insurance or leave wills . . . are people who conceive of themselves, however unconsciously, as part of a great biological stream. Just as something of their ancestors lives on in them, so will something of them live on in their children . . . or in their people, their race, their community—for childless people, too, conduct their lives and try to arrange their postmortem affairs with concern for how the great stream is going to flow on. Most people, historically, have *not* lived their lives as if thinking, "I have only one life to live." Instead, they have lived as if they are living their ancestors' lives and their offsprings' lives and perhaps their neighbors' lives as well. They have seen themselves as inseparable from the great tide of chromosomes of which they are created and which they pass on. The mere fact that you were only going to be here a short time and would be dead soon enough did not give you the license to try to climb out of the stream and change the natural order of things. The Chinese, in ancestor worship, have literally worshipped the great tide itself, and not any god or gods. For anyone to renounce the notion of serial immortality, in the West or the East, has been to defy what seems like a law of nature. Hence the wicked feeling—the excitement!—of "If I've only one life, let me live it as a ————!" Fill in the blank, if you dare.

And now many dare it! In *Democracy in America* de Tocqueville (the inevitable and ubiquitous de Tocqueville) saw the American sense of equality itself as disrupting the stream, which he called "time's pattern": "Not only does democracy make each man forget his ancestors, it hides his descendants from him, and divides him from his contemporaries; it continually turns him back into himself, and threatens, at last, to enclose him entirely in the solitude of his own heart." A grim prospect to the good Alexis de T.—but what did he know about . . . *Let's talk about Me!*

De Tocqueville's idea of modern man lost "in the solitude of his own heart" has been brought forward into our time in such terminology as *alienation* (Marx), *anomie* (Durkheim), the *mass man* (Ortega y Gasset), and *the lonely crowd* (Riesman). The picture is always of a creature uprooted by industrialism, packed together in cities with people he doesn't know, helpless against massive economic and political shifts—in short, a creature like Charlie Chaplin in *Modern Times,* a helpless, bewildered, and dispirited slave of the machinery. This victim of modern times has always been a most appealing figure to intellectuals, artists, and architects. The poor devil so obviously needs *us* to be his Engineers of the Soul, to use a term popular in the Soviet Union in the 1920's. We will pygmalionize this sad lump of clay into a *homo novus,* a New Man, with a new philosophy, a new aesthetics, not to mention new Bauhaus housing and furniture.

But once the dreary little bastards started getting money in the 1940's, they did an astonishing thing—they took their money and ran! They did something only aristocrats (and intellectuals and artists) were supposed to do—they discovered and started doting on *Me*! They've created the greatest age of individualism in American history! All rules are broken! The prophets are out of business! Where the Third Great Awakening will lead—who can presume to say? One only knows that the great religious waves have a momentum all their own. Neither arguments nor policies nor acts of the legislature have been any match for them in the past. And this one has the mightiest, holiest roll of all, the beat that goes... *Me*... *Me*... *Me*... *Me*...

Sex and Violence

Swingers ascending to Heaven through group sex

VII
chapter

The Perfect Crime

(This piece was first published in December 1973, two months before the kidnapping of Patty Hearst.)

REMEMBER THE OLD IDEA OF THE PERFECT CRIME? THE wife kills her husband by hitting him over the head with a frozen leg of lamb. Then she puts the leg of lamb in the stove and sets the temperature at 450 degrees. When the detective comes by to investigate the murder, she takes the murder weapon out of the oven and garnishes it with parsley and mint sauce and puts it on a Spode platter and serves it to the detective. The detective himself devours and digests the evidence! And eliminates it! The wife—the widow—has only to tote up in her mind the fortune that will be coming her way as soon as her husband's will is probated. How cool! How clever! She scores big! leaves not a trace! is never caught!—the Perfect Crime.

The criminal mind has come a long way since then. Not up, not down; just a long way. Consider the Perfect Crime of the 1970's:

On July 17, 1972, a twenty-two-year-old hair stylist sham-
pooed his own hair and hot-combed it down over his forehead
and ears into a John Denver bob, put on a groovy shirt striped
with an intricate leaf-repeat pattern and a pair of bell-bottoms
with fine chalk-and-pin stripes picking up the tones of the shirt,
and walked into a suburban bank near Richmond, Virginia, with
a 12-gauge shotgun. He fired two blasts into a wooden door to
show he meant business. He took nine women and one man as
hostages and herded them into a back room. He spent about five
minutes terrifying them and about four hours trying to charm
them with jokes and the story of his life. He offered them steak
dinners.

"The bank's paying for it!" he said, casting himself in the role
of Tyrone Power as Jesse James.

He was disappointed when they asked for pizzas and beer instead, but he got these Low Rent items for them anyway by
shouting orders to the bank officials and policemen waiting outside. He also ordered $500,000 in cash and a 1972 white Lincoln
Continental to drive away in. He ordered full television and radio coverage of all events, especially the loading of the money
into the trunk of the Lincoln. Said conditions having been met,
he put down the shotgun, said goodbye to the hostages, and
emerged from the bank smiling and waving to the TV cameras
and talking a mile a minute into the microphones, right up until
the moment when federal officers grabbed him. He put up no
struggle at all. They ushered him into the back seat of the white
Lincoln Continental, the very one with the half million in the
trunk, and drove him off to jail. He was still smiling and waving
as the car pulled off.

What on earth, one may ask, could be "perfect" about any such
zany, feckless, giddy, goofy attempt at extortion? Nevertheless, it
was a casebook example of the Perfect Crime of the 1970's, which
is: taking hostages.

Taking hostages is the common core of many different crimes
peculiar to the late 1960's and the 1970's: the more than two hun-

dred airplane hijackings since November 1967; most of the prison riots of the same period, such as the Attica uprising; much of the political terrorism, such as the kidnappings at the 1972 Olympics and in Uruguay; and many attempted bank robberies, such as the incident in Stockholm in which two convicts named Olsson and Olofsson kept four hostages in a bank vault for six days.

Most of the Hostage Takers have been people at the ends of their ropes in struggles against what they regard as the enormity of "the system." Moreover, they seem to think that if they can beat the system, they can also deal with more traditional frustrations, i.e., those involving class, love, and money. One of the most sensational of the airplane hijackings was pulled off by an Italian-born U.S. Marine named Raffaele Minichiello. He took his hostages from Los Angeles to Rome in a wild trip that involved many stops and several changes of crew. Minichiello had grown up in the United States but had never learned English properly and felt like a hopelessly awkward Italian country boy (class); felt too gauche to ask American girls out on dates (love); was decorated for bravery while fighting in Vietnam, only to discover that (by his count) he had been euchred out of $200 in the G.I. savings plan (money); drank six beers and broke into a PX, stole an even $200 worth of merchandise; passed out nearby; was cleared by a local civil judge who simply threw the case out; felt elated; rushed to his commanding officer to bring him the good news; was astounded to hear the C.O. start dictating to his secretary orders for a court-martial, felony level, which would ruin his service career (((((((((((((the unbeatable freaking system!)))))))))))))))))).

So what does the modern Master Criminal do? He *takes hostages*. Ostensibly he takes hostages in order to achieve some goal at the end of the line, but in many cases even the internal logic is bananas. Minichiello said his plan was to hijack a plane to Italy, then hide in the countryside and live off the land like a guerrilla. Palestinian and Uruguayan terrorists take hostages ostensibly to call attention to their causes and gain sympathy. The effect, quite predictably, is the opposite, so far as sympathy is concerned, even among true believers. But so what? The master criminal does not really take hostages in order to accomplish such goals. He dreams up such goals in order to Take Hostages. The formula is turned around: the means justify the end.

With one stroke the Hostage Taker creates his own society, his own system: in the bank vault, in the Olympic quarters, in the airplane, in the prison courtyard. On his own small scale the Hostage Taker accomplishes the classic coup d'état as described by Machiavelli: the sudden, short-term use of terror, cold steel, and bloodletting, if necessary, in order to gain respect—then the long charm course . . . to turn respect into love, thereby making it easy to govern. On the face of it, it is astonishing how often hostages come away from their ordeal describing the Hostage Taker as "nice," "considerate," even "likeable," as in the case of both Minichiello and the groovy hair stylist. A female hostage named Kristin Enmark left the Stockholm bank vault on a stretcher waving to one of the Hostage Takers, Clark Olofsson, telling him, "We'll see each other again!" and informing one and all that he had been kind, hadn't harmed her in the slightest, hadn't been as big a threat as the police, in fact. A psychiatrist immediately explained that she was suffering from shell shock, like a line soldier who has been at the front too long, and was repressing her actual feelings as a "defense mechanism." Is the same to be said of the twenty-nine American passengers and airline crewmen who were held hostage by Palestinian terrorists in Jordan for almost a month and who, *after being freed,* sent a telegram to Israel's Prime Minister Golda Meir saying: "We wish to affirm that our guards treated us humanely and always did their utmost to protect us against harm and to meet our basic needs"—and urging her to give fresh consideration to the Arab cause in Palestine? Thirteen of the twenty-nine signers were Jews.

Far from being a "defense mechanism," such examples are a grand-scale display of a phenomenon well known to police detectives. One of the techniques of the "third degree" involves the Goon & the Nice Guy. The suspect is put into an interrogation room with two detectives, one of whom plays the role of the violent goon while the other plays the nice guy who seeks to protect him. In a remarkably short time, a few hours, in fact, the victim may form an emotional attachment to the Nice Guy, his "protector," and pour out his soul. In precisely the same manner, the Hostage Taker may soon have the hearts and minds of his subjects as well as their hides. The hostage responds like a dog. He has an urge not only to obey but to be obliging and ingratiating in the bargain. What a delightful and emboldening new world!—especially if one has been for so long as helpless as a Palestinian radical up against the complexities of Cold War politics or a Uruguayan radical up against the endless exfoliations of American power in South America. No possible "ransom" or "prisoner release" could compare with the ecstasy of this moment—when for a change I have these people whimpering like dogs at my feet!

All at once I am not the lowliest subject but the head of state. I demand to negotiate with chiefs of police, mayors, governors, and I get my wish. I even have support on the outside. Nelson Rockefeller was heavily criticized for not coming to Attica and negotiating directly with the Hostage Taker inmates. Many hijackers have demanded to talk to the President of the United States. One hijacked a plane to Dulles International Airport and demanded "a million dollars from Lyndon Johnson." At the very least I finally cut through the red tape. I put an end to the eternal runaround. I make the System spin to my number. At last the top people are listening to *me* . . . and answering . . . quite politely, too, and with quite a little choke in their miserable voices . . .

Above all: as long as I have my hostages, as long as the drama has not been played out, I have the ultimate certification that my new status is real and true—that in the most modern sense my class position is secure: *I am a celebrity!* My existence fills the very atmosphere of the city, the state, the nation. As long as Olsson and Olofsson had their hostages in the Stockholm bank vault, Sweden's national election campaign (one of the more crucial since World War II) came to a halt. Who had time for politics, what with O. & O.'s World on TV around the clock? Nor does my celebrity status end with the event itself. Not necessarily! Minichiello became a hero in Italy and served only a year and a half in jail. He appeared continually on television and in magazines. He was signed up for a book and the leading role in an Italian Western. More impressive, he rated the best tables at all the smart restaurants near the Via del Babuino. His troubles with the chicks were over. Marriage proposals were passed in under his door. Movie actresses thrilled to his courage and good looks in the daily pictorials. *Children want my autograph! Everybody loves me!*

At Attica we Hostage Takers custom-ordered our news coverage. For example, we asked for, and got, Tom Wicker of *The New York Times* and he was obliging. He wrote about us as if we were all Prometheuses in noble deathlock with the forces of repression in a battle for the soul of man. As journalism it was pretty embarrassing stuff—but not half bad as a back rub for the boys in Cellblock D!

The groovy at the suburban bank also custom-ordered his news coverage, asking for certain local broadcasters by name. He was in a jolly mood from the moment he first heard live coverage of his escapade over a transistor radio. When the television crews arrived, he made the hostages stick their heads out the window to be filmed, then acted as if he had done them another service, of the magnitude of the beer & pizzas. When the police brought up the white Lincoln Continental, as he demanded, he broke into a grin and announced to his subjects: "You see what you can get with a gun!" The more intense the radio and television coverage became, the better the Hostage Taker's mood became. The police chief characterized it as the turning point—the pressure that finally flushed him out smiling and unarmed, beaming, waving to pals & gals everywhere, to fans, subjects, devotees from border to border and coast to coast . . . and now, the star of our show . . . a sunny day, a perfect crime.

VIII

Pornoviolence

"**K**EEPS HIS MOM-IN-LAW IN CHAINS, MEET *KILLS SON AND FEEDS Corpse to Pigs.*"

"Pleased to meet you."

"*Teenager Twists Off Corpse's Head . . . to Get Gold Teeth,* meet *Strangles Girl Friend, Then Chops Her to Pieces.*"

"How you doing?"

"*Nurse's Aide Sees Fingers Chopped Off in Meat Grinder,* meet *I Left My Babies in the Deep Freeze.*"

"It's a pleasure."

It's a pleasure! No doubt about that! In all these years of journalism I have covered more conventions than I care to remember. Podiatrists, theosophists, Professional Budget Finance dentists, oyster farmers, mathematicians, truckers, dry cleaners, stamp collectors, Esperantists, nudists, and newspaper editors—I have seen them all, together, in vast assemblies, sloughing through the wall-to-wall of a thousand hotel lobbies (the nudists excepted) in their shimmering gray-metal suits and pajama-stripe shirts with white Plasti-Coat name cards on their chests, and I have sat through their speeches and seminars (the nudists included) and attentively endured ear baths such as you wouldn't believe. And yet none has ever been quite like the convention of the stringers for *The National Enquirer.*

The Enquirer is a weekly newspaper that is probably known by sight to millions more than know it by name. No one who ever came face-to-face with *The Enquirer* on a newsstand in its wildest days is likely to have forgotten the sight: a tabloid with great inky shocks of type all over the front page saying something on the order of *Gouges Out Wife's Eyes to Make Her Ugly, Dad Hurls Hot Grease in Daughter's Face, Wife Commits Suicide After 2 Years of Poisoning Fail to Kill Husband . . .*

The stories themselves were supplied largely by stringers, i.e., correspondents, from all over the country, the world, for that matter, mostly copy editors and reporters on local newspapers. Every so often they would come upon a story, usually via the police beat, that was so grotesque the local sheet would discard it or run it in a highly glossed form rather than offend or perplex its readers. The stringers would preserve them for *The Enquirer,* which always rewarded them well and respectfully.

One year *The Enquirer* convened and feted them at a hotel in Manhattan. This convention was a success in every way. The only awkward moment was at the outset when the stringers all pulled in. None of them knew each other. Their hosts got around the problem by introducing them by the stories they had supplied. The introductions went like this:

"Harry, I want you to meet Frank here. Frank did that story, you remember that story, *Midget Murderer Throws Girl Off Cliff after She Refuses to Dance with Him.*"

"Pleased to meet you. That was some story."

"And Harry did the one about *I Spent Three Days Trapped at Bottom of Forty-Foot-Deep Mine Shaft and Was Saved by a Swarm of Flies.*"

"Likewise, I'm sure."

And *Midget Murderer Throws Girl Off Cliff* shakes hands with *I Spent Three Days Trapped at Bottom of Forty-Foot-Deep Mine Shaft*, and *Buries Her Baby Alive* shakes hands with *Boy, Twelve, Strangles Two-Year-Old Girl*, and *Kills Son and Feeds Corpse to Pigs* shakes hands with *He Strangles Old Woman and Smears Corpse with Syrup, Ketchup, and Oatmeal* . . . and . . .

. . . There was a great deal of esprit about the whole thing. These men were, in fact, the avant-garde of a new genre that since then has become institutionalized throughout the nation without anyone knowing its proper name. I speak of the new pornography, the pornography of violence.

Pornography comes from the Greek word *"porne,"* meaning harlot, and pornography is literally the depiction of the acts of harlots. In the new pornography, the theme is not sex. The new pornography depicts practitioners acting out another, murkier drive: people staving teeth in, ripping guts open, blowing brains out, and getting even with all those bastards . . .

The success of *The Enquirer* prompted many imitators to enter the field, *Midnight, The Star Chronicle, The National Insider, Inside News, The National Close-up, The National Tattler, The National Examiner.* A truly competitive free press evolved, and soon a reader could go to the newspaper of his choice for *Kill the Retarded! (Won't You Join My Movement?)* and *Unfaithful Wife? Burn Her Bed!, Harem Master's Mistress Chops Him with Machete, Babe Bites Off Boy's Tongue,* and *Cuts Buddy's Face to Pieces for Stealing His Business and Fiancée.*

And yet the last time I surveyed the Violence press, I noticed a curious thing. These pioneering journals seem to have pulled back. They seem to be regressing to what is by now the Redi-Mix staple of literate Americans, mere sex. *Ecstasy and Me (by Hedy Lamarr),* says *The National Enquirer. I Run a Sex Art Gallery,* says *The National Insider.* What has happened, I think, is something that has happened to avant-gardes in many fields, from William Morris and the Craftsmen to the Bauhaus group. Namely, their discoveries have been preempted by the Establishment and so

Utility
workers
Third Avenue
February 1974

thoroughly dissolved into the mainstream they no longer look original.

Robert Harrison, the former publisher of *Confidential,* and later publisher of the aforementioned *Inside News,* was perhaps the first person to see it coming. I was interviewing Harrison early in January 1964 for a story in *Esquire* about six weeks after the assassination of President Kennedy, and we were in a cab in the West Fifties in Manhattan, at a stoplight, by a newsstand, and Harrison suddenly pointed at the newsstand and said, "Look at that. They're doing the same thing *The Enquirer* does."

There on the stand was a row of slick-paper, magazine-size publications, known in the trade as one-shots, with titles like *Four Days That Shook the World, Death of a President, An American Tragedy,* or just *John Fitzgerald Kennedy (1921–1963).* "You want to know why people buy those things?" said Harrison. "People buy those things to see a man get his head blown off."

And, of course, he was right. Only now the publishers were in many cases the pillars of the American press. Invariably, these "special coverages" of the assassination bore introductions piously commemorating the fallen President, exhorting the American people to strength and unity in a time of crisis, urging greater vigilance and safeguards for the new President, and even raising the nice metaphysical question of collective guilt in "an age of violence."

In the years since then, of course, there has been an incessant replay, with every recoverable clinical detail, of those less than five seconds in which a man got his head blown off. And throughout this deluge of words, pictures, and film frames, I have been intrigued with one thing: The point of view, the vantage point, is almost never that of the victim, riding in the Presidential Lincoln Continental. What you get is . . . the view from Oswald's rifle. You can step right up here and look point-blank right through the very hairline cross in Lee Harvey Oswald's Optics Ordinance four-power Japanese telescopic sight and watch, frame by frame by frame by frame by frame, as that man there's head comes apart. Just a little History there before your very eyes.

The television networks have schooled us in the view from Oswald's rifle and made it seem a normal pastime. The TV viewpoint is nearly always that of the man who is going to strike. The last time I watched *Gunsmoke,* which was not known as a very violent Western in TV terms, the action went like this: The Wellington agents and the stagecoach driver pull guns on the badlands gang leader's daughter and Kitty, the heart-of-gold saloonkeeper, and kidnap them. Then the badlands gang shoots two Wellington agents. Then they tie up five more and talk about shooting them. Then they desist because they might not be able to get a hotel room in the next town if the word got around. Then one badlands gang gunslinger attempts to rape Kitty while the gang leader's younger daughter looks on. Then Kitty resists, so he slugs her one in the jaw. Then the gang leader slugs him. Then the gang leader slugs Kitty. Then Kitty throws hot stew in a gang member's face and hits him over the back of the head with a revolver. Then he knocks her down with a rock. Then the gang sticks up a bank. Here comes the marshal, Matt Dillon. He shoots a gang member and breaks it up. Then the gang leader shoots the guy who was guarding his daughter and the woman. Then the marshal shoots the gang leader. The final exploding bullet signals The End.

It is not the accumulated slayings and bone crushings that make this pornoviolence, however. What makes it pornoviolence is that in almost every case the camera angle, therefore the viewer, is with the gun, the fist, the rock. The pornography of violence has no point of view in the old sense that novels do. You do not live the action through the hero's eyes. You live with the aggressor, whoever he may be. One moment you are the hero. The next you are the villain. No matter whose side you may be on consciously, you are in fact with the muscle, and it is you who disintegrate all comers, villains, lawmen, women, anybody. On the rare occasions in which the gun is emptied into the camera— i.e., into your face—the effect is so startling that the pornography of violence all but loses its fantasy charm. There are not nearly so many masochists as sadists among those little devils whispering into one's ears.

In fact, sex—"sadomasochism"—is only a part of the pornography of violence. Violence is much more wrapped up, simply, with status. Violence is the simple, ultimate solution for problems of status competition, just as gambling is the simple, ultimate solution for economic competition. The old pornography was the fantasy of easy sexual delights in a world where sex was kept unavailable. The new pornography is the fantasy of easy triumph in a world where status competition has become so complicated and frustrating.

Already the old pornography is losing its kick because of overexposure. In the late thirties, Nathanael West published his last and best-regarded novel, *The Day of the Locust,* and it was a terrible flop commercially, and his publisher said if he ever published another book about Hollywood it would "have to be *My Thirty-nine Ways of Making Love by Hedy Lamarr.*" He thought he was saying something that was funny because it was beyond the realm of possibility. Less than thirty years later, however, Hedy Lamarr's *Ecstasy and Me* was published. Whether she mentions thirty-nine ways, I'm not sure, but she gets off to a flying start: "The men in my life have ranged from a classic case history of impotence, to a whip-brandishing sadist who enjoyed sex only after he tied my arms behind me with the sash of his robe. There was another man who took his pleasure with a girl in my own bed, while he thought I was asleep in it."

Yet she was too late. The book very nearly sank without a trace. The sin itself is wearing out. Pornography cannot exist without certified taboo to violate. And today Lust, like the rest of the Seven Deadly Sins—Pride, Sloth, Envy, Greed, Anger, and Gluttony—is becoming a rather minor vice. The Seven Deadly Sins, after all, are only sins against the self. Theologically, the idea of Lust—well, the idea is that if you seduce some poor girl from Akron, it is not a sin because you are ruining her, but because you are wasting your time and your energies and damaging your own spirit. This goes back to the old work ethic, when the idea was to keep every able-bodied man's shoulder to the wheel. In an age of riches for all, the ethic becomes more nearly: Let him do anything he pleases, as long as he doesn't get in my way. And if he does get in my way, or even if he doesn't . . . well . . . we have *new* fantasies for that. *Put hair on the walls.*

"Hair on the walls" is the invisible subtitle of Truman Capote's book *In Cold Blood.* The book is neither a who-done-it nor a will-they-be-caught, since the answers to both questions are known from the outset. It does ask why-did-they-do-it, but the answer is soon as clear as it is going to be. Instead, the book's suspense is based largely on a totally new idea in detective stories: the promise of gory details, and the withholding of them until the end. Early in the game one of the two murderers, Dick, starts promising to put "plenty of hair on them-those walls" with a shotgun. So read on, gentle readers, and on and on; you are led up to the moment before the crime on page 60—yet the specifics, what happened, the gory details, are kept out of sight, in grisly dangle, until page 244.

But Dick and Perry, Capote's killers, are only a couple of Low Rent bums. With James Bond the new pornography reached dead center, the bureaucratic middle class. The appeal of Bond has been explained as the appeal of the lone man who can solve enormously complicated, even world problems through his own bravery and initiative. But Bond is not a lone man at all, of course. He is not the Lone Ranger. He is much easier to identify than that. He is a salaried functionary in a bureaucracy. He is a sport, but a believable one; not a millionaire, but a bureaucrat on an expense account. He is not even a high-level bureaucrat. He is an operative. This point is carefully and repeatedly made by having his superiors dress him down for violations of standard operating procedure. Bond, like the Lone Ranger, solves problems with guns and fists. When it is over, however, the Lone Ranger leaves a silver bullet. Bond, like the rest of us, fills out a report in triplicate.

Marshall McLuhan says we are in a period in which it will become harder and harder to stimulate lust through words and pictures—i.e., the old pornography. In the latest round of pornographic movies the producers have found it necessary to introduce violence, bondage, torture, and aggressive physical destruction to an extraordinary degree. The same sort of bloody escalation may very well happen in the pure pornography of violence. Even such able craftsmen as Truman Capote, Ian Fleming, NBC, and CBS may not suffice. Fortunately, there are historical models to rescue us from this frustration. In the latter days of the Roman Empire, the Emperor Commodus became jealous of the celebrity of the great gladiators. He took to the arena himself, with his sword, and began dispatching suitably screened cripples and hobbled fighters. Audience participation became so popular that soon various *illuminati* of the Commodus set, various boys and girls of the year, were out there, suited up, gaily cutting a sequence of dwarf and feebles down to short ribs. Ah, swinging generations, what new delights await?

chapter

**The Boiler Room and
the Computer**

SUCH HEAVING!
Such groaning!
Such peeling squealing
Biting sticking
Ramming jamming
Gobble licking
Nuzzling guzzling
Coconut ilia
Rut-boar grunting
Skotophilia
Lapping gashing
Crinkly chasms
Prescribed therapeutic spasms—
—and if there is any justice up in heaven, Dr. Freud has been
assigned a corner apartment with one of those little concrete bal-
conies or "terraces," of the Collins Avenue condominium-tower
variety, rigged out with a telescope and an infrared X-ray attach-

ment that enables him to look down through every roof and every ceiling in the United States . . . day or night, into overstore massage parlors on lower State Street as easily as the flimsiest cinder-block motel room, even into the utter darkness of the Lido East movie theater . . . so that he may enjoy every last jerk, shudder, and gush that his remarkable brain—clinically dead since 1939—continues to trigger in our time . . . I doubt that there is another man in history whose ideas, unaided by any political apparatus, have directly influenced the behavior of so many people in the generations immediately following his death. Darwin and Marx are in the running perhaps; perhaps Zoroaster, if what little has been recorded of his history is to be believed; possibly Rousseau, although it is difficult to say that his influence was direct. No, on second thought the good doctor stands alone . . . on his condominium terrace, I like to think . . . clapping his hands together like a child with mittens, as he so often did when he was praised during his lifetime.

Now, the complex and subtle parts of Freud's theory, featuring elaborate literary conceits and marvelous leaps of analogy, have scarcely made a dent on posterity. What has sunk in so deeply has been a single, simple notion of his concerning sexuality. This notion bears none of the elegant nomenclature which he loved so much, nothing on the order of *the Oedipus complex* (he adored italics), *libido,* or *Ego&Id&Superego.* In fact, he gave it no name at all, since it grew out of a mere habit of thought whose importance he never recognized.

During Freud's university years (the late 1870's and early 1880's) young enthusiasts in the fuzzier disciplines, such as psychology, liked to borrow terminology from the more rigorous and established field of mechanical physics. The borrowed terms became, in fact, metaphor; and metaphor, like a shrewd servant, has a way of ruling its master. Thus Freud wound up with the idea that libido or sexual "energy," as he called it, is a pressure that builds up within a closed system to the point where it demands release, as in a steam engine. "It seems that an accumulation of narcissistic libido over and above a certain level becomes intolerable," he would say. "It depends on the *amount* of undischarged libido that a person can hold freely suspended . . ." "The next disturbance of the shifting forces will cause symptoms to develop, unless he can yet find other outlets for his pent-up libido . . ." In short, a head of steam. When it builds up high enough, the foreman (the ego) either opens up some workable valve and lets it out—or it's hamburger heaven for one and all in the boiler room! (in the form of obsessional neurosis, hysteria, or much worse).

Such, in brief, is the history of the piece of conventional wisdom that today animates what is known as the "sexual revolution": namely, the belief that regular release of the steam, in the form of guilt-free orgasm, is essential to a healthy psyche and a healthy society.

Over the past four years women's-liberation theorists have criticized Freud as a man who put forth ideas as if they applied equally to men and women but who actually thought like a man. And they are quite correct. Yet in the same breath they (along with sexologists such as the Drs. Reuben, Comfort, and Brothers, the spouses O'Neill, and Madame Hollander & Co.) proceed to press Freud's Boiler Room Axiom on their sisters. Stand up like a man! Go forth! Get it on! Take the sexual initiative! Be free! Let the steam out! Get well soon!

Meanwhile, on other fronts it is much the same. The pornographers argue (with many intellectuals in accord) that their product is society's "safety valve"; the potential rapist or other twisted sex geek discharges his steam manually in the gloaming of the peep-show booth or at home with the aid of a stroke magazine (the cathartic theory) . . . Or, on a more sophisticated level, that the stroke magazine or "erotic art"—to use the term they prefer—creates a liberating atmosphere in which the individual is encouraged to clean out his (and, presumably, her) valves and pipes without the hazards of guilt and repression (the therapeutic theory). Likewise, the massage parlor, as one learns regularly

Lexington Avenue and 62nd Street

in magazine and television interviews, "helps save marriages, because a man can come here and get what he needs when he can't get it at home. Anyway, it beats masturbation." Swinging, or group sex, becomes the answer to the problem of "different and ever-changing sexual urges. To think that the traditional marriage partnership can take care of them is unrealistic. Isn't it healthier for couples to join groups where variety is the norm and you can shed your inhibitions and let your sexual energy flow freely?"

Lovely . . . Freud's Boiler Room Axiom—on all fronts! You can't make the pressure go away, friends—so make the most of it! Tune up the machine! Oil the works! Go with the flow!

In the midst of all the solemn and dedicated groin spasms that have ensued . . . arrives one as yet tiny but disturbing note. It is this: over the past twenty years, thanks to the refinement of techniques such as the stereotaxic needle implant, neurophysiologists have begun to study the actual workings of the brain and central nervous system. These investigators find no buildups of "pressure" or "energy," sexual or otherwise, for the simple reason that the central nervous system is not analogous to an engine. They regard it as more like an electronic circuit, such as a computer or a telephone system. Millions of neurons fire continually, and the electrical energy within the system remains constant. Behavior is determined, instead, by which lines are open and what messages get through. According to this model, what is the effect of pornography—or group sex—or "massages"—or orgasmic regularity? Far from being a safety valve releasing energy that has built up inside the system, any such pastime is more like an input that starts turning on the YES gates . . . to the point where its message *(Sex!)* closes out all others and takes over the entire circuit . . .

In one way, of course, the neurophysiologists are doing exactly what Freud did a century ago: they are adopting the most fashionable machine metaphor of their own day—namely, computer terminology. And perhaps they, as well, stand to delude themselves. But they also have one advantage. Freud began and ended with a hypothesis; with the techniques available in his time he could go no further. The neurophysiologists are at least able to proceed down the chain of hypothesis, deduction, observation, and verification. And so far they have found nothing to indicate that the entire body of psychoanalysis has any more to offer on the subject of sexuality than the Lights Out league manual for boys concerning what to do with your hands when the Cosmic Itch gets aggravated (Answer: Sit on them).

Freud's biographers tell us that his preoccupation with sex began in earnest when he psychoanalyzed himself and discovered that throughout his boyhood he had lusted for his mother. *Sex!* How irresistible it is to speculate that if the lad had but run around the block a few times in a spirited fashion whenever the evil impulse seized him and taken cold showers regularly, each afternoon, for a few weeks, as it suggests in the manual, the tenor of life today in the United States, and throughout the West, might be radically different. Cooler and less humid, in any event; so much less heaving groaning peeling squealing biting sticking ramming jamming gobble licking nuzzling guzzling und so weiter, meine Freunde.

Manners, Decor, and Decorum

The Debutante in Blue Jeans

chapter

X

Funky Chic

BY OCTOBER OF 1969 FUNKY CHIC WAS FLYING THROUGH London like an infected bat, which is to say, silently, blindly, insanely, and at night, fangs afoam ... but with an infallible aim for the main vein ... much like the Sideburns Fairy, who had been cruising about the city since 1966, visiting young groovies in their sleep and causing them to awake with sideburns running down their jawbones. Funky Chic, as I say ... So it happened that one night in a club called Arethusa, a favorite spot of the London *bon ton,* I witnessed the following: A man comes running into the Gents and squares off in front of a mirror, removes his tie and stuffs it into a pocket of his leather coat, jerks open the top four buttons of his shirt, shoves his fingers in under the hair on top of his head and starts thrashing and tousling it into a ferocious disarray, steps back and appraises the results, turns his head this way and that, pulls his shirt open a little wider to let the hair on his chest sprout out, and then, seeing that everything is just so, heads in toward the dining room for the main event. This dining room is a terrific place. It has just been done over in the white plaster arches and cylindrical lamps of the smart restaurant decor of that time known as Expense Chit Trattoria. In the grand salon only the waiters wear white shirts and black ties. The clientele sit there roaring and gurgling and flashing fireproof grins in a rout of leather jerkins, Hindu tunics, buckskin shirts, deerslayer boots, dueling shirts, bandannas knotted at the Adam's apple, love beads dangling to the belly, turtlenecks reaching up to meet the muttonchops at midjowl, Indian blouses worn thin and raggy to reveal the jutting nipples and crimson aureolae underneath ... The place looks like some grand luxe dining room on the Mediterranean unaccountably overrun by mob-scene scruffs from out of *Northwest Passage, The Informer, Gunga Din,* and *Bitter Rice.* What I was gazing upon was in fact the full fashion splendor of London's *jeunesse dorée,* which by 1969, of course, included everyone under the age of sixty-seven with a taste for the high life.

Funky Chic came skipping and screaming into the United States the following year in the form of such marvelous figures as the Debutante in Blue Jeans. She was to be found on the fashion pages in every city of any size in the country. There she is in the photograph ... wearing her blue jeans and her blue work shirt, open to the sternum, with her long pre-Raphaelite hair parted on top of the skull, uncoiffed but recently washed and blown dry with a Continental pro-style dryer (the word-of-mouth that year said the Continental gave her more "body") ... and she is telling her interviewer:

"We're not having any 'coming-out balls' this year or any 'deb parties' or any of that. We're fed up with doing all the same old things, which are so useless, and seeing the same old faces and dancing to so-called society bands while a lot of old ladies in orange-juice-colored dresses stand around the edges talking to our parents. We're tired of cotillions and hunt cups and smart weekends. You want to know what I did last weekend? I spent

The aging groovy with the popular George McGovern Alpine Mountain Climber Rope-throw hairdo

last weekend at the day-care center, looking after the most beautiful black children . . . and *learning* from them!"

Or as a well-known, full-grown socialite, Amanda Burden, said at that time: "The sophistication of the baby blacks has made me rethink my attitudes." Whereupon she described herself as "anti-fashion."

Anti-fashion! Terrific. Right away anti-fashion itself became the most raving fashion imaginable . . . also known as Funky Chic. Everybody had sworn off fashion, but somehow nobody moved to Cincinnati to work among the poor. Instead, everyone stayed put and imported the poor to the fashion pages. That's the way it happened! For it was in that same year, 1970, that Funky Chic evolved into its most exquisite manifestation, namely, Radical Chic (if I may be forgiven for saying so) . . . Socialites began to give parties for the Black Panthers (to name but one of many groups) at their homes, from Park Avenue to Croton-on-Hudson. Which is to say, they began to bring exotic revolutionaries into their living rooms and thereby achieved the ultimate in Funky Chic interior decoration: live black bodies.

It was at this point that fashion, on the one hand, and politics, ideology, and philosophy, on the other, began to interlock in a most puzzling way. The fashion of Radical Chic swept not only socialites but also intellectuals and cultivated persons of every sort in the years 1968–70. The situation began to contradict the conventional assumption of historians, which is that fashion is but the embroidery of history, if that. It is true that Radical Chic would have never become a fashion if certain political ideas and emotions had not already been in the air. But once Radical Chic became fashionable, it took on its own momentum. It had the power to create political change on its own—i.e., many influential people who had been generally apolitical began to express support for groups like the Panthers.

The conventional wisdom is that fashion is some sort of store-front that one chooses, honestly or deceptively, to place between the outside world and his "real self." But there is a counter notion: namely, that every person's "real self," his psyche, his soul, is largely the product of fashion and other outside influences on his status. Such has been the suggestion of the stray figure here and there; the German sociologist Rene Konig, for example, or the Spanish biologist Jose M. R. Delgado. This is not a notion that is likely to get a very charitable reception just now, among scholars or readers generally. If the Bourbon Louises may be said to have lived in the Age of Absolutism, we now live in the Age of Egalitarianism (with the emphasis on the *ism,* if one need edit). Even people who lend themselves to the fashion pages, the people whose faces run through *Vogue, Bazaar, Harper's Bazaar & Queen* and *Town & Country* like a bolt of crisp white-glazed chintz, are not going to be caught out today talking about fashion in terms of *being fashionable.* They talk instead of ease, comfort, convenience, practicality, simplicity, and, occasionally, fun and gaiety (for others to share). Right now I am looking at a page of photographs in *Bazaar* of a woman named Venetia Barker, a young English matron whose husband owns a stable of horses and a fleet of helicopters. She tells how two or three times a week she flies her own canary-yellow helicopter from their country home in Wiltshire to their townhouse in London in order to go antique hunting. Twice a week she flies it to Worcestershire to go horseback riding in the fox hunts. She speaks of the helicopter as a time-saving convenience, however, and of fox hunting in terms of mental hygiene: two days a week with horse & hound beats the psychiatrist any time in coping with the pressures of a busy modern life. "During the day," she says, "I wear what's most practical," items such as a Regency coachman's cape with three huge layers of flapping red overlaps about the shoulders plus leather pants by Foale and Tuffin of London. At night she changes "into something quite simple," which turns out to be outfits such as a black tunic gown by the good Madame Gres, slashed on the sides to reveal a floor-length scarlet slip and cross-laced black drawstrings, and surmounted at the bosom by a filigree diamond necklace with an emerald pendant the size of a Brazil nut. Con-

venience, health, practicality, simplicity . . . none of which means
that the woman is being hypocritical or even cagy. She is merely
observing a convention, a fashion taboo that is common to people
at every level of income and status today.

The curious thing is that the same taboo makes fashion an
even touchier subject for scholars. Louis Auchincloss once observed that academic writers seem to find the courage to write
about society, in the sense of fashionable society, only from a great
distance—either from across an ocean or across a gulf of a century or more in time, and preferably both. "Why can we find a
hundred professors eager to explore the subtleties of the court of
the Empress Theodora," he asks, "and not one to plumb the
depths of a party given by Perle Mesta?" He also remarked, quite
aptly, I would say, that nothing offers a more revealing insight
into the character of the high tide of American capitalism than
the social life of Newport in the 1890's—"a crazy patchwork of
borrowed values financed on a scale that would have made the
Sun King stare"—and to this day the one serious study of it is by
a Frenchman (Paul Bourget).

Auchincloss is a novelist, of course, and ever since the time of
Richardson and Fielding, some 230 years ago, novelists have been
drawn to fashion as an essential ingredient of realistic narration.
This was out of sheer instinct and not theory. Early in the game
they seemed to sense that fashion is a code, a symbolic vocabulary
that offers a subrational but instant and very brilliant illumina-
tion of the characters of individuals and even entire periods, especially periods of great turmoil. And yet novelists who have
dwelled on fashion in just this way have usually been regarded in
their own time as lightweights—"trivial" has been the going
word—scarcely even literary artists, in fact; even those who eventually have been judged to be the literary giants of their eras. Dr.
Johnson dismissed Fielding as a minor, trivial, unserious to the
very end. He could not understand how any serious writer could
wallow so contentedly in the manners and mores, the everyday
habits, of so many rascals, high and low. Saint-Beuve continually

compared Balzac to people like antique dealers, sellers of women's clothes, and—this was one of his favorites—the sort of down-at-the-heel petty bourgeois doctors who make house calls and become neighborhood gossips. Balzac was not regarded as a major writer until after his death; he was not even invited to join the French Academy.

In our own time I don't have the slightest doubt but that Evelyn Waugh will eventually stand as England's only major novelist of the twentieth century (oh, all right, him and Lawrence). But during the last decade of his life his stock sank very low; so low, in fact, that he seemed finally to downgrade himself, judging by the opening chapter of *The Ordeal of Gilbert Pinfold*. In his writing he immersed himself so deeply in the fashions of his times that many critics regarded him as a snob first and an artist second. (I recall one English reviewer who was furious because Waugh had the hero of his *Men at Arms* trilogy, Guy Crouchback, describe his father's funeral mainly in terms of how correctly everyone had dressed for the event despite the fact that it was wartime and the services were out in the country.) John O'Hara's reputation has undergone a similar deflation over the past fifteen years. As for Louis Auchincloss, more than once he has set in motion characters who pursue the lure of Wall Street & Wealth & Family & Men's Club in the most relentless manner—only to see critics complain that the character is not believable: People don't conduct their lives that way any more. Auchincloss notes with some annoyance that they are saying "don't" when what they mean is "shouldn't."

Auchincloss identifies the moral objection that underlies the taboo as follows. At the very core of fashionable society exists a monstrous vulgarity: "the habit of judging human beings by standards having no necessary relation to their character." To be found dwelling upon this vulgarity, absorbed in it, is like being found watching a suck 'n' fuck movie. It is no use telling people you were merely there as a detached observer in the age of *Deep Throat;* in the case of fashion, too, the grubbiness rubs off all the same, upon scholars no less than novelists, socialites, and gossip columnists. Unlike a Balzac or a Gogol, the scholar seldom treats fashion as an essential ingredient of history. Instead, he treats it as comic relief, usually set apart from the narrative in an archly written chapter with a coy title such as "Bumpkins and Brummels: From Country Fair to Mayfair."

TODAY, IN THE AGE OF FUNKY CHIC EGALITÉ, FASHION IS A much more devious, sly, and convoluted business than anything that was ever dreamed of at Versailles. At Versailles, where Louis XIV was installed in suites full of silver furniture (later melted down to finance a war), one could scarcely be *too* obvious. Versailles was above all the City of the Rich. Hundreds of well-to-do or upward-hustling families had quarters there. The only proper way to move about the place was in sedan chairs borne by hackmen with straining trapeziuses. Any time anyone of high social wattage gave a party, there would be a sedan-chair traffic jam of a half hour or more outside his entry way as the true and original *jeunesse dorée,* in actual golden threads and golden slippers, waited to make the proper drop-dead entrance.

One has only to compare such a scene with any involving the golden youth of our own day. I recommend to anyone interested in the subject the long block, or concourse, known as Broadway in New Haven, Connecticut, where Elm Street, York Street, Whalley and Dixwell Avenues come together. This is near the heart of Yale University. Twenty years ago, at Elm and York, there was a concentration of men's custom-tailoring shops that seemed to outnumber all the tailors on Fifth Avenue and Fifty-seventh Street put together. They were jammed in like pearls in a box. Yale was still the capital of collegiate smart dressing. Yale was, after all, the place where the *jeunesse dorée* of America were being groomed, in every sense of the word, to inherit the world; the world, of course, being Wall Street and Madison Avenue. Five out of every seven Yale undergraduates could tell whether the button-down Oxford-cloth shirt you had on was from Fenn-Feinstein, J. Press, or Brooks Brothers from a single glance at your shirt front; Fenn-Feinstein: plain breast pocket; J. Press: breast pocket with buttoned flap; Brooks Brothers: no breast pocket at all. Today J. Press is still on the case, but others of the heavenly host are shipping out. Today a sane businessman would sooner open a souvlaki takeout counter at Elm and York than a tailor shop, for reasons any fool could see. On the other side of the grand concourse, lollygagging up against Brooks Health and Beauty Aids, Whitlock's, and the Yale Co-op, are the new Sons of Eli. They are from the same families as before, averaging about $37,500 gross income per annum among the non-scholarship students. But there is nobody out there checking breast pockets or jacket vents or any of the rest of it. The unvarying style at Yale today is best described as Late Army Surplus. Broadway Army & Navy enters heaven! Sons in Levi's, break through that line! that is the sign we hail! Visible at Elm and York are more olive-green ponchos, clodhoppers, and parachute boots, more leaky-dye blue turtlenecks, pea jackets, ski hats, long-distance trucker warms, sheepherder's coats, fisherman's slickers, down-home tenant-farmer bib overalls, coal-stoker strap undershirts, fringed cow-poke jerkins, strike-hall blue workshirts, lumberjack plaids, forest-ranger mackinaws, Australian bushrider mackintoshes, Cong sandals, bike leathers, and more jeans, jeans, jeans, jeans, jeans, more prole gear of every description than you ever saw or read of in a hundred novels by Jack London, Jack Conroy, Maxim Gorky, Clara Weatherwax, and any who came before or after.

OF COURSE, THIS HAPPENS TO BE PRECISELY WHAT AMERICA'S most favored young men are wearing at every other major college in the country, so that you scarcely detect the significance of it all until you look down to the opposite end of the concourse, to the north, where Dixwell Avenue comes in. Dixwell Avenue is

The Pimpmobile Pyramid-heel Platform Soul Prince Albert Coat Got-to-get-over look of Dixwell Avenue

the main drag of one of New Haven's black slums. There, on any likely corner, one can see congregations of young men the same age as the Yalies but . . . from the bottom end of the great greased pole of life, as it were, from families whose gross incomes no one but the eligibility worker ever bothered to tote up. All the young aces and dudes are out there lollygagging around the front of the Monterey Club, wearing their two-tone patent Pyramids with the five-inch heels that swell out at the bottom to match the Pierre Chareau Art Deco plaid bell-bottom baggies they have on with the three-inch-deep elephant cuffs tapering upward toward the "spray-can fit" in the seat, as it is known, and the peg-top waistband with self-covered buttons and the beagle-collar pattern-on-pattern Walt Frazier shirt, all of it surmounted by the midi-length leather piece with the welted waist seam and the Prince Albert pockets and the black Pimpmobile hat with the four-inch turn-down brim and the six-inch pop-up crown with the golden chain-belt hatband . . . and all of them, every ace, every dude, out there just *getting over* in the baddest possible way, come to play and dressed to slay . . . so that somehow the sons of the slums have become the Brummels and Gentlemen of Leisure, the true fashion plates of the 1970's, and the Sons of Eli dress like the working class of 1934 . . .

. . . a style note which I mention not merely for the sake of irony. Just as Radical Chic was a social fashion that ended up having a political impact—so did Funky Chic. Radical Chic helped various Left causes. Funky Chic hurt them. So far as I know, no one has ever recorded the disruption that Funky Chic caused within the New Left. (Remember the New Left?) In 1968, 1969, and 1970 the term "counterculture" actually meant something. In those wild spitting hot-bacon days on the campus "counterculture" referred to what seemed to be a fast-rising unity of spirit among all the youth of the nation, black and white, a new consciousness (to use a favorite word from that time) that was mobilizing half the country, the half that was now under twenty-five years old (to use a favorite statistic from that time), under the banner of revolution or something not far from it. Yet at that very moment the youth of the country were becoming bitterly divided along lines of class and status. The more the New Left tried to merge them in a united front, the more chaotic and out of the question the would-be coalition became.

Fashion was hardly one of the root causes of this division—that is another, longer story. But fashion was in many cases the cutting edge. Fashion brought out hopeless status conflict where there was no ideological conflict whatsoever. In 1969 I went to San Francisco to do a story on the young militants who were beginning to raise hell inside the supposedly shockproof compound of Chinatown. I had heard of a sensational public meeting held by a group called the Wah Ching, who were described as a supergang of young Chinese who had been born in Hong Kong, who immigrated to the United States with their parents in the mid-sixties, who couldn't speak English, couldn't get an education, couldn't get jobs, who were ready to explode. They held a public meeting and threatened to burn down Chinatown, Watts-style. So I came on into Chinatown, cold, looking for the Wah Ching. Right away, on the street corners, I see groups of really fierce-looking young men. They've got miles of long black hair, down to the shoulders, black berets, black T-shirts, black chinos, dirty Levi's, combat boots. These must be the dread Wah Ching, I figured. So I worked up my nerve and started talking to some of them and right away I found out they were not the Wah Ching at all. They were a group known as the Red Guard, affiliated at that time with the Black Panthers. Not only that, they were not lower-class Hong Kong-born Chinese at all but American-born. They spoke English just like any other Americans; and most of them, by Chinatown standards at least, were middle-class. But they said they were allied with the Wah Ching and told of various heavy battles the Wah Ching were going to help them out in.

It took me about two weeks, but I finally arranged a meeting with one of the main leaders of the Wah Ching themselves. We were going to meet in a restaurant, and I arrived first and was sitting there going over all the political points I wanted to cover. Finally the man walks in—and I take one look and forget every political question on the list. He has on a pair of blue slacks, a matching blue turtleneck jersey with a blue shirt over it and a jacket with a leather body and great fluffy flannel sleeves, kind of like a suburban bowling jacket. This man does not add up. But mainly it is his hair. After all the ferocious long black hair I have been seeing in Chinatown—his is chopped off down to what is almost a parody of the old Chinatown ricebowl haircut. So the first magnificent question I heard myself blurting out was: "What happened to your hair!"

There was no reason why he should, but he took the question seriously. He spoke a very broken English which I will not attempt to imitate, but the gist of what he said was this:

"We don't wear our hair like the hippies; we don't wear our hair like the Red Guards. We are not a part of the hippies; we are not a part of the Red Guards; we are not a part of anything. We are the Wah Ching. When we got to this country, those guys you were talking to out there, the ones who now call themselves the Red Guard, those same guys were calling us 'China Bugs' and beating up on us and pushing us around. But now we're unified, and we're the Wah Ching and nobody pushes us around. So now they come to us and tell us they are the Red Guard and they've got the message and Chairman Mao and the Red Book and all that. They'll give us the message and the direction, and we can be the muscle and the power on the street and together we will fight the Establishment.

"Well, the hell with that. We don't need any ideological benefactors. Look at these guys. Look at these outfits they're wearing. They come around us having a good time playing poor and saying, 'Hey, brother.' Look at those berets—they think they're Fidel Castro coming out of the mountains. Look at the Can't-Bust-'Em overalls they got on, with the hairy gorilla emblem on the back and the combat boots and the olive-green socks on you buy two-for-29-cents at the Army-Navy Store. They're having a

Butterfly T-shirts and Continental baggies with elephant bell cuffs

good time playing poor, but we are the ones who have to *be* poor. So the hell with that and the hell with them."

Here were two groups who were unified ideologically—who wanted to fight the old clan establishment of Chinatown as well as the white establishment of San Francisco—and yet they remained split along a sheerly dividing line, an instinctive status line, a line that might even be described by the accursed word itself, "fashion." This example could be multiplied endlessly, through every instance in which the New Left tried to enlist the youth of the working class or of the slums. There never was a "counterculture" in the sense of any broad unity among the young—and this curious, uncomfortable matter of fashion played a part over and over. I never talked to a group of black militants, or Latin militants, for that matter, who didn't eventually comment derisively about the poorboy outfits their middle-class white student allies insisted on wearing or the way they tried to use black street argot, all the *mans* and *cats* and *babies* and *brothers* and *baddests*. From the very first, fashion tipped them off to something that was not demonstrated on the level of logic until much later: namely, that most of the white New Lefters of the period 1968–70 were neither soldiers nor politicians but simply actors.

The tipoff was not the fact that the middle-class whites were dressing *down* in order to join their slum-bound brethren. The issue was not merely condescension. The tipoff was that when the whites dressed down, went Funky Chic, they did it *wrong*! They did it *lame*! They never bothered to look at what the brothers on the street were actually wearing! They needed to have their coats pulled! The New Left had a strictly old-fashioned conception of life on the street, a romantic and nostalgic one somehow derived from literary images of *proletarian* life from before World War II or even World War I. A lot of the white college boys, for example, would go for those checked lumberjack shirts that are so heavy and woolly that you can wear them like a jacket. It was as if all the little Lord Byrons had a hopeless nostalgia for the proletariat of about 1910, the Miners with Dirty Faces era, and never mind the realities—because the realities were that by 1968 the real hard-core street youth in the slums were not into lumberjack shirts, Can't Bust 'Ems, and Army surplus socks. They were into the James Brown look. They were into ruffled shirts and black-belted leather pieces and bell-cuff herringbones, all that stuff, macking around, getting over, looking sharp . . . heading toward the high-heeled Pimpmobile *got to get over* look of Dixwell Avenue 1976. If you tried to put one of those lumpy mildew mothball lumberjack shirts on them—those aces . . . they'd *vomit*.

FOR YEARS THE SHEERLY DIVIDING LINE WAS A SINGLE ITEM OF clothing that is practically synonymous with Funky Chic: blue jeans. Well-to-do Europeans appreciated the chic of jeans—that primitive rawness; that delicious lubricous grip on the gourd and the moist skinny slither up into all the cracks and folds and fissures!—long before Americans. Even in the early fifties such special styles as London S.W. 5 New Wave Habitat Bentwood Movie Producer Chic and South of France Young Jade Chic and Jardins du Luxembourg Post-Breathless Chic all had at their core: blue jeans. Cowboy Chic, involving blue jeans and walking around as if you have an aluminum beer keg between your thighs, has been popular among young Paris groovies for at least fifteen years. Well-to-do whites in America began to discover the raw-vital reverse-spin funk thrill of jeans in the early sixties. But until recently any such appeal was utterly lost on black or any other colored street aces and scarlet creepers. Jeans were associated with funk in its miserable aspects, with Down-and-Out, bib overalls, Down Home, and I'm Gonna Send You Back to Georgia. Jeans have just begun to be incorporated in the Ace or Pimp look, thanks to certain dramatic changes in jeans couture: such as the addition of metal studwork, bias-cut two-tone swirl mosaic patterns, windowpane welt patterns, and the rising value of used denim fabric, now highly prized for its "velvet hand" (and highly priced, just as a used Tabriz rug is worth more than a new one). In other words, the aces will now tolerate jeans precisely because they have lost much of their funk.

Well-to-do white youths still associate jeans in any form and at any price with Funk, however, and Funky Chic still flies and bites the main vein and foams and reigns. The current talk of a Return to Elegance among the young immediately becomes a laugh and a half (or, more precisely, the latest clothing industry shuck) to anyone who sets foot on a mainly white American campus, whether Yale or the University of California at San Diego. A minor matter perhaps; but today, as always, the authentic language of fashion is worth listening to. For fashion, to put it most simply, is the code language of status. We are in an age when people will sooner confess their sexual secrets—much sooner, in many cases—than their status secrets, whether in the sense of longings and triumphs or humiliations and defeats. And yet we make broad status confessions every day in our response to fashion. No one—no one, that is, except the occasional fugitive or spy, such as Colonel Abel, who was willing to pose for years as a Low Rent photographer in a loft in Brooklyn—no one is able to resist that delicious itch to reveal his own picture of himself through fashion.

Goethe once noted that in the last year of his reign Louis XVI took to sleeping on the floor beside his enormous royal bed, because he had begun to feel that the monarchy was an abomination. Down here on the floor he felt closer to the people. How very . . . funky . . . Well, I won't attempt any broad analogies. Nevertheless, it demonstrates one thing. Even when so miserable a fashion as Funky Chic crops up . . . stay alert! use your bean!

chapter XI

Honks and Wonks

"**D**JA DO DA CHEM-YET?"

Dja do da chem-yet?

—this being the voice of a freshman on the campus of C.C.N.Y. at 139th Street and Convent Avenue the other day asking the question: "Have you done the chemistry assignment yet?" The irony of it is that here is a boy who will probably *do da chem* and God knows how many other assignments extremely well and score about a 3.5 academic average over four years and then go to law school at N.Y.U. and get his LL.B—and then for some reason he can't quite figure out, he never does land the great glistening job he was thinking of at Sullivan & Cromwell or Cravath Swain & Moore. Instead, he ends up in . . . *the neighborhood,* on the south side of Northern Boulevard in Bayside, Queens, in an office he shares with a real-estate man, an old friend of his from here in Bayside—which some of the local wiseacres call Brayside, because of all the "Brooklyn" and "Bronx" accents you hear here in Queens now—

Whaddya mean it's his voice? He's upgraded the *da* with *the* by now, hasn't he? And hasn't he replaced the *r*'s he's been dropping all these years—well, a few of them, anyway: "This is the *first* house we *evuh* owned. We have a *gahden* an my wife is the *gahdneh . . ."*

. . . here in Brayside . . .

The same day, in the little exotic knickknacks boutique on the ground floor of Henri Bendel, on Fifty-seventh Street just west of Fifth: a nice New York girl home from St. Timothy's, St. Tim's, the boarding school in Maryland. She and a girlfriend of hers are walking around town *checking boys,* among other things. It's true! They can tell just by looking at him whether a boy goes to an Eastern prep school or not. Not only that, they can tell *which prep school,* usually St. Paul's or Hotchkiss or Groton or Exeter or Andover, or whatever; just by checking his hair and his clothes. And *certainly* if they can get just one sentence out of him—

—like this gorgeous boy here, a tall milk-fed stud in a Brooks yellow shirt and tasseled loafers fumbling over a Cameroons egret-skin hassock with his tweedy-thatchy Prince Charles hanging over his brow and— He's Exeter, or possibly Andover. That is obvious immediately from the tie. His tie is tied properly at the throat, but the ends are slung over his left shoulder, after the fashion. And their eyes meet, and then his eyes shift to her shoes, naturally, and then he looks into her eyes again, into her soul, as it were, and says:

"Those are real Guccis, aren't they?"

Bliss! It's all there! Past, present, future! Certified! The Guccis, of course, being her loafers, bought at Gucci's, 699 Fifth Avenue, with the authentic Gucci gold chain across the tongue and not any of the countless imitations of the Gucci loafer. A shorthand! A very metonymy! For the whole Eastern boarding-school thing, but more than that—the *honk!* He has it, the Eastern boy's boarding-school *honk,* lifting every vowel—*Those are real Guccis, aren't they?*—up over the roof of his palate and sticking them into his nose and honking them out without moving his lower jaw. And there in one sentence he has said it all, announced that he belongs in the world of the New York *honks,* of the honks who rule and possess all and who every day sound the secret honk of New York wealth and position; the nasal knighthood of the Bobby Kennedys, the Robert Dowlings, Huntington Hartfords, Nelson Rockefellers, Thomas Hovings, Averell Harrimans—for in New York the world is sheerly but secretly divided into the *honks* and the wonks*—*Dja do da chem-yet?*—and this fumbling milk-fed Exeter stud will carry a C-plus straight to Wall Street or mid-Manhattan, for he is *one of us,* you understand—

Very ironic—the way New Yorkers at every class level delighted for years in *My Fair Lady* on stage and screen. *My Fair Lady,* of course, is the musical version of Shaw's play *Pygmalion,* about a linguistics professor, Henry Higgins, turning a Cockney flower seller into a lady of Society by upgrading her accent. That silly, stuffy English class system!—whereupon we all settled back and just enjoyed the Cinderella love story. It was just as well. It is probably a good thing that no Henry Higgins has come along to wake up New York to the phonetic truth about class and status in this city . . .

---

*Honk is a term of Eastern prep-school derivation, connoting both the nasal quality of the upper-class voice and its presumably authoritative sound, commanding obedience, like the horn of a large 1936 Packard. It is not to be confused with "honkie," the black slang word for "white man," which is apparently a variation on a still older slang word, "hunky," originally a term of opprobrium for Hungarian immigrants to the U.S. "Wonk" is an Eastern prep-school term referring to all those who do not have the "honk" voice, i.e., all who are non-aristocratic. There is some conjecture that the term is derived in the natural Anglophile bias of Eastern social life from the English adjective "wonky," meaning unsteady, shaky, feeble, awry, off. In current use, however, "wonk" is a vague, all-inclusive term, closely akin to the terms "wog" and "wop," which are sometimes used at Eastern prep schools to refer to all the rest of humanity.

I HAVE BEEN TALKING TO A MAN WHO COULD DO IT IF HE chose to, however—Professor Marshall D. Berger of C.C.N.Y. Berger is one of the country's leading geographical linguists, one of those extraordinary people, like Henry Lee Smith of the old radio days, who can listen to a man for thirty seconds and tell what part of what state he was raised in. Berger is a big husky man. He is fifty-five years old and has lived in New York since he was thirteen. His family moved from Buffalo to Liberty Avenue in the East New York section of Brooklyn, where the kids all thought it was odd to the point of *weird* that he said things like *core*-respondence instead of *cah*-respondence and referred to the well-known game of *go'f* as *gawlf.* He wrote an honors thesis at C.C.N.Y. in 1941 on "The Sources of New York Speech," and then a doctoral dissertation at Columbia on "American-English Pronunciations of Russian-born Immigrants." And so for the past three decades he has been doomed by his own specialty to listen, day in and day out, to New Yorkers unconsciously confessing their ancestry, their status, their social yearnings, every time they open their struggling lips.

"This is a very sensitive area you're asking me about," he tells me. "The first thing you'll notice is that people in New York always invent euphemisms when they get on the subject of speech. They don't want to talk about ethnic background or class. So they invent euphemisms. They talk about a 'Brooklyn' accent or a 'Bronx' accent, when what they're really talking about are working-class and lower-middle-class accents found all over the city. Years ago, when Brooklyn was still a big farm, they talked about the 'Bowery' accent."

Berger's own voice sounds to me like Radio Announcer Rugged, if you know that sound. In any case—

"Even the newspapers, at this late date, observe the taboo. I remember the *Post*'s biographical sketch of a local college president. 'His speech betrays his Bronx origins,' they wrote. They were talking about 'lower class' and I suppose the readers get the point, but everyone observes the taboo.

"The same goes for 'New York accent.' Nothing pleases most New Yorkers more than to be told that they've 'lost their New York accent.' This is ironic, on the face of it, since New York is one of the great cosmopolitan centers of the world. But what they're thinking about, of course, is class. 'I've lost my lower-class accent,' they're thinking. Incidentally, people who tell you 'I've lost this or that accent' or 'I really don't have any accent any more' are almost invariably fooling themselves. What they've done in most cases is change a couple of obvious vowels or consonants—they may have changed their pronunciation of *example* from *ex-EHM-ple,* which is lower class or lower middle class, to ex-AM-ple, or something of the sort—but they've seldom changed their basic pattern. Even broadcasters."

The glorious New York accent!

In 'is town deh's nuh-uhn doin at da foist of da week, so I was lookin at a likka avatisement an I bought a bah-uhl an relaxed.

All this glorious dropping of *r*'s and *g*'s and *d*'s and muffing of the "voiceless linguadental fricative" (turning the *th* sound into *d*) and reducing vowels until they almost disappear—the usual explanation has been the waves of immigrants to New York in the 1890's and early 1900's. New York, of course, had had waves of immigrants before. But they were chiefly northern Europeans, Irish, German, Dutch, English, and they were middle as well as lower class. The new immigrants were chiefly from Eastern and Southern Europe, and they were lower class; Italians, Ukrainians, Poles, Russians, Greeks, Eastern European Jews, speaking Italian, Greek, Yiddish, Russian, and other Slavic tongues. Part of the "New York accent" that developed was a blend of the new speech patterns with English words.

For example, of the new tongues only Greek had the *th* sound. The result was millions of New Yorkers saying *wid* for *with* and *dis* for *this*. Or: in Yiddish a *t* in the middle of a word, like *winter,* was pronounced much more emphatically than it is in English. To this day, the New Yorker who says win-*t*a or fundamen-*t*al is usually someone from a home where Yiddish was spoken. Likewise, the heavily accented *g,* as in *sin-ga* for *singer* and *Lon Gy-land* for *Long Island*. Other innovations were in rhythm. Some of the most flamboyant came from Southern Italian and Sicilian lower-class speech, with the old . . . *So I says to my brudd'n'law, "Awriiide, so whaddya wan me to do, I says to him, whaddya* whad-dya *or sump'm?"*

These were all foreign flavors coming into New York English, but many of the elements of the "New York accent" had been here for years before the 1890 wave of immigrants; notably, such things as *dis* for *this* and *foist* for *first*. Berger's theory hits on a far more subtle point. Namely, street masculinity. Here were millions of working-class people massed into lower Manhattan, and their sons fell into the street life. On the street the big thing was physical competition, even if it was only stickball or, today, rock 'em games of basketball on a concrete slab shooting for a basket with a metal backboard and a rim with no net on it . . . In any case, the emphasis was always on the large muscles.

For a start, the street thing led to rapid speech in which words are swallowed whole, *r*'s are dropped, vowels are reduced to the vanishing point, and even some hard consonants disappear. A three-syllable word like *memory* gets reduced to one and a half or less: *m'm'r. Bottle* becomes *bah-uhl, little* becomes *lih-uhl.* A pronunciation like *lih-uhl* is what is known as a glottal stop, in which the double *t* is replaced by what is in fact a miniature cough. It is common in New York City, although in England, among the lower classes, the glottal stop sometimes replaces *p*'s and *k*'s as well as *t*'s. Street masculinity has also led New Yorkers to carry their tongues low in their mouths like dockworker's forearms. The result is some heavy handling of many consonants: *t*'s and *d*'s get dropped or mushed around. Most people's speech patterns are set between the ages of five and fifteen, and they are not likely to revamp them in any thorough way after that without something on the order of dramatic training. Often not even that will do it. A boy growing up on the street may unconsciously scorn the kind of delicate muscle play an upper-class boy learns in articulating words. The fancy work with the tip of the tongue in pronouncing *portraiture,* for example, may strike him as effete, even girlish. It seems to me that when it comes to prep-school *honks* like Averell Harriman, or Thomas Hoving—well, it doesn't matter how many worlds they have conquered or how old they are. As soon as they open their mouths, a bell goes off in the brains of most local-bred New York males: *sissy.* Here are a coupla kids who woulda got *mashed* in the street life. John Lindsay (St. Paul's) suffered continually from this disability when he was mayor of New York; also Bobby Kennedy (Milton Academy). Kennedy took the edge off his Bugs Bunny delicacy with public displays of masculinity of various sorts.

Women generally try much harder than men in New York to escape from the rock-bottom working-class accents, but they are often unaware of where the true . . . *honk-wonk* divide lies. They tug and pull on their accents, but often only get them into a form that the upper orders can laugh at in musical comedies. There is the musical-comedy working girl, for example, who is always saying,

Oh, Mr. Steiiiiiiin, I had such a foiiiiin toiiiime, pronouncing the *i* as if she has wrapped it around a perfume bottle. In real life she is not a lower-class girl at all, but lower middle class.

The lower-middle-class girl who says *toiiiime* may also be aware, instinctively, that the muscle-bound tongue accounts for much of the lower-class sound. So she begins using her tongue in a vigorous way in pronouncing all sorts of things—only she overdoes it. She shoves her words all over the place but still doesn't hit them cleanly. This is the common phenomenon of the beautiful girl—"but she ruined it as soon as she opened her mouth." Here she is with her Twiggy eyes, Eve Nelson curly look, a wool jersey mini from Plymouth's, patent-leather pseudo-Guccis from A. S. Beck—and a huge rosy lingual blob rolling around between her orthodontic teeth.

The *oi* sound in *toiiiime,* by the way, is not to be confused with the so-called Brooklyn *oi* sound comedians always used to mimic:

"Da oily boid gets da woim," "She read da New Yoik *Woild,*" "She lives on Toity-toid Street." These are all examples of dropping *r*'s and substituting *oi* for the *er* sound. Today you are only likely to hear it from older working-class people, such as some of the old cab drivers. This is one lower-class sound that dates back well before 1890 and is not even a peculiarly New York pronunciation. The same sound—it is actually closer to *ui* than *oi*, more like *fuist* than *foist*—can be heard today in two Southern port cities, Charleston, S.C., and New Orleans, among both upper- and lower-class people. A century ago upper-class New Yorkers used the same pronunciation, only with a slightly flutier intonation. About half a century ago upper-class New Yorkers began changing their pronunciation of *first* from a fluty *fuist* to a Boston or English *fuhst.*

This is all *r*-dropping, as I say, and it is one of the most subtle and vital matters in phonetic social climbing in New York. This is where strivers get caught out. The New Yorker who has risen above *wid* and ex*ehm*ple and even *toiiiime* and aspires to true bourgeois status will next start to replace all the *r*'s he or his family have been dropping all his life.

The *fi*rst pahty I went to was in my senya yea*rr*—and so forth—not realizing that in the upper orders he envies everybody is busy dropping *r*'s like mad, in the ancient English mode.

Many New Yorkers have taken conscious pains to upgrade their accents socially and confidently believe that they now have the neutral accent of a "radio announcer." Three pronunciations almost invariably give them away: *owies* for *always* (lower-class *l*-dropping); *fo'ud* for *forward* (dropping the *r* and the *w*); frank*foot*er for *frankfurter* and *footer moment* for *for the moment* (lower-class *r*-dropping).

"The fact is," Berger tells me, "that a person who tries to change one or two elements in his speech pattern may end up in worse shape than he thought he was in to begin with. His original pattern may not be prestigious, but it may be very good in terms of its internal arrangements, and he may succeed only in upsetting the equilibrium. Frankly, I like to hear people like Vito Battista and Jimmy Breslin talk. They have working-class accents and they don't care who knows it. They're very confident, that's the main thing. 'Dis is da way I tawk an dis is da way I'm *gonna* tawk, an you betta lissen.' A person's speech pattern is bound up with so many things, his personality, his role, his ambitions, that you can't deal with in isolation or simply in terms of some 'ideal.' "

Yes . . . but! . . . suppose your ideal is to get your daughter's picture on the first page of the Wedlock Section of the Sunday *Times,* and not in one of those scrimy little one-paragraphers at the bottom of the page, either—you know those little one-paragraphers, the ones hog-to-jowl up against the Arnold Constable ad with a little headlinette over the paragraph saying

HORLEK-KLOTKIN

Suppose you're after the pole position, up at the top of the page, with a big three-column picture all downy silk with backlighting rising up behind her head like a choir of angels are back there singing and glowing, and a true headline proclaiming:

SATTERTHWAITE-KLOTKIN
BETROTHAL ANNOUNCED

One option is to do what Mrs. Bouvier did with her daughter Jacqueline. Namely, pack her off to a Virginia boarding school, whence she can return to New York bearing what the press chooses to call a "little girl voice" but which is known in the secret *honk* world as the "Southern 45-degree Upturn," in which your daughter turns her mouth up 45 degrees at either end, then her eyeballs, and says:

Ah you rilly an ahkitect
Ah you rilly a docta?

Ah you rilly a senata?

And travel *fuhst* class forever after.

THE BRITISH BROAD *A* HAS NO SOCIAL CACHET IN NEW YORK.
Quite the opposite, in fact. Unless it is being used by an Englishman, it is taken as a sign of striving for a naïve or Schrafft's Mid-afternoon gentility. The great hangout of the American broad *a*
used to be a vast L-shaped Schrafft's restaurant that had entrances on both Madison Avenue and East Fifty-eighth Street.
The most genteel-looking matrons imaginable, dressed up in
outfits such as three-piece peach wool suits with fur trim at the
collars and cuffs and hats with enormous puffed-up crowns of
cream-colored velvet, over apricot-colored hair, used to gather in
Schrafft's throughout the afternoon. Much of the conversation
had to do with stock quotations. You would hear the ladies say to
one another:

"Ackshewly, I think Automatex is rahther pahst its peak."

"Oh, I know. It opened higher this mawning, but ahfter hahlf
an hour it was down by two."

Such a conversation indicated that they had spent the morning
in the spectator seats of the midtown street-level offices of the
brokerage houses, in the board rooms, as they are called. This
does *not* indicate wealth and position. For one thing, the E.S.A.
(Eastern Socially Attractive) way for a woman to refer to her investments (if at all) is to make them seem as if they are *way out
there* somewhere and she hasn't the vaguest idea what happens to
them. For another, the old parties who hang out in the spectator
seats of the midtown brokerage houses are referred to by the brokerage house employees as "board-room bums."

For still another, Schrafft's was not exactly the most prestigious place for a woman to eat. But eating at Schrafft's did have
a certain secret beauty to it: the much underestimated beauty of
American Comfort. The ladies' typical meal at Schrafft's was a

cheeseburger, coffee, and a sundae. But such sundaes! Sundaes with towers of ice cream and nuts and sauces and fudge and maraschino cherries of a quality and buttery beauty such as the outside world has never dreamed of! And the secret art of the mid-afternoon at Schrafft's was *pacing* and the *final shape*. It was not enough merely to consume the sundae. No, the idea was to pace one's consumption along with everyone else's at the table, so that one did not finish up more than thirty seconds ahead of anyone else and, furthermore, so that one's very last bite—*the final shape*—would be a *perfect miniature* of the original cheeseburger or of the original sundae, with precisely the same proportions of hamburger, cheese, and bread, or of ice cream, whipped cream, sauce, nuts, and fruit dressing, as the cheeseburger or the sundae had at the outset when it was first served. And . . . they were *served so beautifully!* The waitresses at Schrafft's, who seemed to be women who had immigrated from Europe as adults, were perhaps the most considerate and sensitive waitresses in the history of America. They understood, tacitly, from long observation, about the final shape and its importance. If a woman had eaten two thirds of her cheeseburger but had eaten it incorrectly, so that the bread and the hamburger were left in the form of a perfect final shape, as if there were a perfect mini-burger two inches in diameter on the plate, except that the cheese was all gone—she had only to ask for more cheese, and one of these waitresses, these angels, these nurses sent by Our Lady of Comfort, would take the cheeseburger, two thirds eaten, back to the kitchen and have a perfectly proportioned two-inch slab of cheese placed—but not merely *placed*—no!—*broiled!*—*broiled onto the remains!*—and they would bring it back with a smile, as if to say, "There! We understand, you and I!"

"Oh, I cahn't thank you enough, my dear!"

Now there, I submit, is Beauty. It is not, however, prestige.

The true social competitors among New York's older women gather earlier, about 1 p.m., for the Status Lunch, and the accents are quite different. The Status Lunch is a peculiarly New York institution in this country, although the same thing goes on in a less manic way in Paris and London. At the Status Lunch women who have reached the upper social orders gather during the week so that they may demonstrate and celebrate their position. They may be at the top through family background or marriage or other good fortune. In any case, they are mostly in their late thirties or in their forties or early fifties, starving themselves to near perfection in order to retain . . . *the look* . . . with just a few piano wires showing in their necks and forearms and the backs of their hands, owing to the deterioration of the body packing. Or perhaps they have begun to let themselves go into that glorious creamy Camembert look in which the flesh on the shoulders and the upper back and the backs of their arms looks like it could be shaped with a butter knife. They are Pucci'd and Gucci'd up to their temporal fossae, Pucci in the dress, Gucci in the shoes and handbag—the Pucci-Gucci girls!—yes. They start pulling into Status Lunch restaurants in the East and West Fifties, such as La Grenouille, Lutèce, Orsini's, about 1 p.m. and make a great point of calling the maître d' by his first name, which at La Grenouille is Paul, then peer into that ocher golden mirrored gloom to case the important tables, which are along the walls in the front room, by way of weighing the social weight of today's gathering, as it were. Then they suck in their cheeks—near perfection—and begin the entrance, looking straight ahead, as if they couldn't be more oblivious of who else is there, but waiting, hopefully, for the *voice*—

Dah-ling dah-ling dah-ling.

There it is!—the *dah-ling* voice, a languid weak baritone, not a man's voice, you understand, but a woman's, *The New York Social Baritone*, like that of a forty-eight-year-old male dwarf who just woke up after smoking three packs of Camels the day before, and then the social kisses, right out in the middle of the restaurant, with everybody locking heads, wincing slightly from the concentration on not actually pressing the lips, which would smudge the lipstick, or maybe even the powder covering the electrolysis lines above the lips, with the Social Baritone *dah-ling* voices beginning to bray softly in each other's ears, like an ensemble of cellos—*we are all here!* This voice cannot be achieved without some ten or fifteen years of smoking cigarettes and drinking whiskey or gin, which literally smoke-cures and pickles the vocal cords and changes them from soprano to the golden richness of baritone. It takes, on the average, at least 13,000 cigarettes over a ten-year period. In pronunciation, the *dah-ling* voice seeks to set itself off from both the urgency (what's going to hit the fan next?) of the lower-class female voice and the usual efficiency (must pronounce everything *correctly)* of the middle-class female voice with a languor and a nasal *honk,* connoting ease, leisure, insouciance. Two techniques are the most vital: dropping *r*'s, as in *dahling,* and pronouncing most accented vowels with a sigh thrown in, particularly the *a*'s and *o*'s, as in—

Dahling, I caaaaan't [but not *cahnt*]. I just did the Mehhhht and, you know, the sets were stunnnnnning, Myron le Poove I think he is, but it was the most boooooooring-sawt-of-thing—with the vowels coming out of the nose in gasps as if she is going to run out of gas at any moment.

And *yet!* She has worked on this voice for ten years, producing her deep rich pre-cancerous vocal cords, but it gives off the deadly odor: *parvenu.* The *dahling* voice, heard so often at Status Lunches and country weekends and dinner parties where two wineglasses are used, is almost invariably that of the striver who has come upon the upper-class *honk* voice too late in life. She has picked up a number of key principles: the nasality, the languor, the oiliness, the *r*-dropping. But she does not understand the underlying principle, which is historical. Her attention is fixed upon New York, and as a result her voice takes on a New York theatrical manner, a staginess, in the Tallulah Bankhead mode, which is show-business upper class, not *honk* upper class. The certified *honk* upper-class woman in New York has her attention fixed, phonetically although unconsciously, on Boston and the Richmond-Charleston social axis of the South.

The secret here, as among New York male *honks,* is the boarding school. The outstanding girls' boarding schools are oriented, socially, toward the nineteenth-century upper-class traditions of Boston and the South, which, until after World War I, had far more social clout than the upper-class world of New York. Miss Hall's, Miss Porter's, Westover, and Dana Hall are all girls' boarding schools where an old Boston upper-class tradition dominates, just as Foxcroft (Jackie Kennedy's school), Madeira, Chatham Hall, Garrison Forest, and St. Catherine's are still schools where the Richmond-Charleston tradition dominates. New York girls bring back the Boston or Southern sound in a somewhat crude form, but nevertheless it is not a New York sound. It is neither a street sound nor a theatrical sound nor an English sound. Its components are nasality, languor, oiliness, *r*-dropping—but with shorter, clearer, more open vowels than the *dahling* voice. If the girl has gone to a Southern school, like Jackie Kennedy, she will tend to have a soft, childish voice. If she has gone to a "Boston" school, the speech will be much brisker and yet still languid and oily, as if lubricated ball bearings were pouring out of both nostrils.

In the nineteenth century, the New York upper classes were much more directly influenced by Boston and the South. Boston overshadowed New York in many phases of business, finance, and law and was unquestionably New York's social superior in the area of Culture and the Arts. The New York upper classes had close ties with the Southern upper classes because of the shipping trade. Southern planters came to New York continually for financing, and packet boats loaded with cotton came to New York on the way to England. About 1940, linguists at C.C.N.Y. made recordings of the voices of old New Yorkers, people in their seventies and eighties, most of them upper-middle-class, in order to get an idea of what speech patterns were like in New York in the nineteenth century. They tended to speak in a medley of Boston and Southern accents. One old party reminisced about an old structure on Twenty-third Street as "the old struk-cha on Twenty-thuid Street," with *struk-cha* a combination of the clipped Boston accent of *struk* and the Boston *r*-dropping of *cha;* and *Twenty-thuid* a case of Southern-style upper-class *r*-dropping, substituting a diphthong vowel sound, *ui,* for the standard *er* sound in *third.* Socially, New York was considered an exciting but crude town, and New York's upper classes felt the sense of inferiority and preferred to sound as if they came from some better spot. Even today some *honks* still use the Southern upper-class pronunciation of *thuid* for *third,* although most have shifted over the past half century to a more Bostonian *thuhd.* They still drop the *r* in any case.

Boys as well as girls, of course, learn the *honk* voice in prep school, and the same principle applies: the voice should suggest a languor that will separate one from the lower orders. The lower jaw is moved much less than in ordinary speech and the words are lifted up over the palate and secreted through the nose rather than merely blurted out of the mouth. The rigidity of the jaw may resemble an affliction to a person who has never watched someone speak this way before. In fact, the E.S.A. accent that is often heard on the North Shore of Long Island in communities such as Huntington and Oyster Bay is known as Locust Valley Lockjaw. The same voice is known in Riverdale as Spotted Bostonian. Socially ambitious people in Riverdale may even try to keep their voices up by spending their summers in the select vacation communities of the Boston upper orders on the Maine shore.

Honk voices may fall anywhere in a range from Boston-Honk to New York-Honk. Leaning toward the Boston-Honk would be the late Bobby Kennedy (Milton Academy), Averell Harriman (Groton), the late Christian Herter (St. Paul's), and the late John F. Kennedy (Choate). The worst liabilities of the *honk* voice to a politician, quite aside from the class overtones, are the monotony and the delicacy and weakness brought about by this sort of voice's emphasis on languor and refinement. Bobby Kennedy, like his brother John, had great difficulty in conventional oratory from a rostrum. His voice was trained in delicacy rather than strength and tended to turn shrill at the very moment when the heavy chord should have been hit. He always sounded like a seventeen-year-old valedictorian with the goslings. In the case of Harriman and Herter, it was the nerve-gas monotony of the *honk* voice that caused them trouble as much as anything else.

The perfect New York *honk* voice is Huntington Hartford's (St. Paul's). Other notable New York *honks:* Nelson Rockefeller and the late Robert Dowling, the real-estate and investment tycoon. Their type of voice has the nasality of the *honk* voice without the delicacy of the same voice as practiced by Bobby Kennedy or even former New York Mayor John Lindsay (St. Paul's). The explanation, most likely, is that both Rockefeller and Dowling went to prep school in the city, Rockefeller at the Lincoln School and Dowling at Cutler. Rockefeller has gradually coarsened his voice for his public appearances. It is a kind of *honk* with a knish jammed in it, although he uses much more a conventional soft *honk* in private conversation. One of the ironies of the 1962 race for governor was that Rockefeller's upper-class voice with a knish in it was so much more effective among Low Rent voters in New York than that of his upper-middle-class opponent, Robert Morgenthau. As a result of his time at Deerfield Academy, Morgenthau's voice had taken on a kind of *honk* subtlety and delicacy that made him, not Rockefeller, sound like the Fauntleroy in the plot.

Lindsay tried to come down off the *honk* accent somewhat by inserting *r*'s where they would ordinarily be dropped, making his speech sound almost middle-class at points. He also referred to St. Paul's as his "high school" from time to time, as if it were nothing more than a kind of Stuyvesant or DeWitt Clinton unaccountably set out in Concord, New Hampshire. This was a laugh and a half to all old "Paulies," who are generally fond of St. Paul's reputation as the most snobbish school in America.

Even Amy Vanderbilt tried to roughen up her female *honk* accent by adding middle-class *r*'s, perhaps in an unconscious rub-off from the various bourgeois commercial interests with which she was involved. In general, the public spotlight tends to make *honks* nervous about their voices, whether they are politicians or performers or merely celebrities. Very few have the self-assurance to just keep pouring it on, the way Roosevelt did:

I hate wooouugggggggghawwwwwwwwwwwggggggghhhhhhhh —meaning *war.*

Boys today at St. Paul's, Groton, Middlesex, Hotchkiss, Deerfield, St. Mark's, St. George's, Exeter, Andover, and the rest of them are strangely goosy about it themselves. They are apparently hung up on the masculinity thing, as they might put it, rather preferring to have both the social certification of the languid, delicate *honk* voice and the ruggedness and virility of various street voices. The upshot has been that they have kept the *honk* voice but picked up the dope argot of Greenwich Village, the Lower East Side, and other lower-middle-class bohemias, studding the most improbable conversations with the inarticulate litany of "like-I-mean-you-know-man" intoned in a kind of Bugs Bunny Bobby Kennedy *honk* spew of lubricated BB's:

Laiike, nyew nyeoow, man, ai mean, Fisha's Island is a groove and a gas compaaaiiihed to Deeah Island and, like, now, ai mean, Wildwood, Nyew Juhsey, is prackly a mindblowagggh . . .

And the whole *honk* world sinks, *wonking,* into a vast gummy Welt-smeared nostalgia for the mud.

XII

chapter

The Street Fighters

TONIGHT, THIRTY MINUTES AGO IN FACT, IT WAS THE SAME thing, same as last night, the usual farce. The fact is, I have never seen a decent street fight in New York. Mexican stand-offs, screaming lulus, belly bumpers, sternum prodders—one debacle after another! An endless supply! But pugnacious? Oh yes. Every man in the street in New York is a fighter, especially from inside a car. The insults! I've lived here for many years and I still can't believe what I hear people call each other. Lame brain! Asshole! Schmuck! Pansy! Fruit basket! Gladiola! Cow! Eggplant! Jungle bunny! They'll say anything. *Asshole* is the going insult this year. Everybody's an asshole. Immediately! Without a moment's notice! Never mind the preliminaries!

This morning, for example, I was riding in a cab turning off Forty-second Street into Madison Avenue, and the driver cuts right behind a man standing in Forty-second Street trying to walk across the street. He cuts so close—for a split second a hand-grenade loop on the fellow's trenchcoat—yes! precisely! a hand-grenade loop!—a hand-grenade loop on the fellow's trenchcoat clinks inside the window next to where I'm sitting. The man is furious. He glowers. Naturally my boy, the driver, lets him have it—immediately! That's the ticket! He sticks his head out the window. He bares his teeth.

"Look where you're going," he says, "you asshole!"

There it is! Asshole!

The man in the trenchcoat can't believe it. He's beside himself. He lifts up his leg. He has a ferocious pair of sideburns and a little trick hat of the Alpine style. He lifts up his leg, like a dog. He kicks the cab in the fender. It makes a hell of a noise. He's kicking and screaming at the same time and thrashing his sideburns around. He shrieks out: "You fucking . . . *guinea!*"

He calls my boy a *guinea*! My boy's name is Segal. It's posted, along with his picture and the cab number, up on the dashboard. Segal says, "Whadjoo say, asshole!"

We're out onto Madison now, but you can still hear the poor devil out in the middle of Forty-second Street screaming out from between his sideburns into the *Weltchaos* . . . "I said youa fucking guinea!"

Now the cabbie turns around to me. I'm his star witness, of course.

"Did you see that asshole?"

I nod, like an idiot . . .

"I'm watching the light! Why can't these assholes watch the light!"

Naturally all this asshole and fucking-guinea business leads to real fights sooner or later. *Then* you should see the street fighters of New York . . . Debacles, as I was saying. Last night, about 8:30, down on Wall Street, or, rather, City Hall Plaza it was, where Park Row, Fulton Street, Lafayette, Centre, Broadway, and the Manhattan end of the Brooklyn Bridge come together. All the hustling studs who have worked late in the law firms and financial houses have drifted up from Wall Street to the plaza to look for cabs. But there are no cabs. Practically nobody takes a cab

down to Wall Street at night, so there are no cabs down here to go home in. Some college student driving a cab part-time at night who isn't rude enough or sly enough yet to talk his way out of a fare to Brooklyn and is coming back empty over the bridge—that is the best you can hope for. The Wall Street studs are roaming around in the darkness with their attaché cases. Every single one has an attaché case. It's no joke! All circling, jockeying for position, there are ten of them, fifteen, twenty. It's windy and cold as hell. There's a madness in the dark: the cab fever. Their eyes are beginning to shine. They're like raccoons. There's one of them there, under the cigar sign. Another one! under the electrolysis sign. Suddenly here's a cab heading down Park Row toward the big bend through the plaza. Everybody springs into action, me included, running, waving, screaming like maniacs. "Cab!" "Taxi!" And the whistles! Oh, Christ! The kind of whistle where you stick two fingers in your mouth. It's bedlam. The battle is on.

Two of them from the other side of Park Row have cut across the concrete center strip. They hit the rear door of the cab at the same time. One has his hand on the handle. The other one bellies in. It's fierce!

"Listen!" the other one says. "I hailed this cab!"

"Hey! Watch it! I got here first!"

"Ohhhhhhh, no!" He throws the little menacing laugh in there. "Take your hand off that door, you asshole!"

"Who are you calling an asshole!"

"You, you little asshole!"

"Whuhh—I'll show you who's an asshole, asshole!"

It's a chorus! A reprise! An opera! A regular Asshole Rigoletto! I'm right on top of them. They're bona fide Wall Street lifers, both of them, out in the middle of the street calling each other asshole four times to the beat. They're both in their mid-forties, I would say. They both have on $35 felt hats with creases down the center, semi-homburg style, the old Wall Street crash helmet. They've both got on terrific overcoats and shirt collars that fit, with nice smooth pink jowls popping out like toothpaste.

They've both got attaché cases in their right hands, the leather lunch pails. That's what gets me: the attaché cases. They won't let go! One of them throws a shoulder block. Right guard on the Hill School Jayvees, 1946! Prep macho! The other one throws a shoulder block.

They're pushing and shoving. One stiff-arms the other one in the face with his left hand—Hotchkiss "B" squad, 1949—and then bangs him over the head with the attaché case with the right. The other one sticks out a left and then bangs *him* over the head with his attaché case. They keep throwing these pathetic lefts and then bringing on that great roundhouse right bolo overhead attaché case to the squash.

Bop!
            Bop!
Bop!
            Bop!

The attaché cases make this little *bop* sound when they hit. They're like two old burlesque comedians hitting each other with pig bladders, with blown-up condoms. They won't let go! They're beating each other's hat into a hell of a wad. They're fierce. They can't raise a bruise, however. The cab is still sitting right there. The driver is a great fat guy. He doesn't budge. He has a ringside seat. He's fascinated, like everybody else.

They're flailing away like a couple of broken fan belts. They're gasping. They're heaving. They're running out of breath. It's ludicrous. They can't say asshole any more. *Assuh* is the way it comes out. Assuh! *Bop!* Assuh! *Bop!* And then *As! Bop . . . As! . . . Bop . . . As! . . .*

All this has lasted maybe thirty seconds. But suddenly they're falling back. They're staggering on their heels like balloon dolls. They're dead on their feet. They've had it. They're gasping for breath. They're in for it now. Twenty years of eating English mixed grills and drinking draft beer in the hofbraus of Wall

Street . . . split-pea soup and salt sticks and real butter and Cheddar and Roquefort and Camembert and vodka-tonic . . . and the arteries are all gunked up until the passage narrows to the size of a syringe opening . . . Ah! those winter vacation days in old St. Croix when the tiger puts on his new paisley swimming trunks from J. Press and looks in the mirror and expands his chest and throws back his shoulders to flatten out the little titties beginning to form on the chest . . . Ummm . . . I really ought to start working out . . . but the old basic muscle structure is still there . . . not a bad build, tiger . . . hell, if I worked out a good hard four weeks . . . I know what, I'll skip lunches and start playing squash at the Barclay Health Club . . . But, oh, God! the credit has just run out, friends!

They're gasping for breath. They're white in the face, blue in the mouth. Their eyes are rolling back. They don't know where the hell they are. The cab driver moves for the first time. Freak this! He's not going to be witness to a double coronary attack and lose a day's pay. Not this boy. He guns off, leaving the two studs blobbing about in the middle of Park Row. They don't know where they are. They're sucking air. But they're still holding on to the attaché cases. Their knuckles are white from it. I'll never forget it. They stagger toward the curb like a couple of rocking druids. They collapse. They're half sitting, half lying in the curb, gasping, heaving, rolling their eyes . . . Intimations of mortality . . . Do I die right here! . . . There's not five feet between them . . . *Assuh* . . . But they're both finished . . . Two tigers . . . with thirty seconds of fight in them . . . A pure farce, in a word . . .

That's it! There's not one tiger in a hundred in New York who is in condition to have a street fight. They're all like those club fighters I used to see at Parker Field in Richmond, Virginia, on Thursday nights. After two rounds they were stroked out on each other's shoulders, marathon-dancing around the ring. Everybody starts yelling and jeering. Fakes! Phonies! Pansies! But that wasn't it. They were out of breath. It was as simple as that. There was no more. Hell, even a young fighter has to run a couple of miles, and hit the heavy punching bag for an hour, every day for a month to go six rounds at full speed. And our tigers of the street . . . They're indecent . . .

NEAR THE ENTRANCE TO BETH ISRAEL HOSPITAL, ON SIX- teenth Street and First Avenue, there's a crowd in the street near the candy store. Ah! a street fight. Everybody is jumping up and down and banging into each other from behind to get a better look. It seems the heavy in the piece, a big Puerto Rican kid, six- teen or seventeen, was picking on some little Irish kid from Stuyvesant Town project, across the street, and then this other lit- tle Irish kid, a skinny little guy, about fourteen, steps in. He's half the big guy's size. They both sound the old cry. Now they're banging away. The Puerto Rican kid is trying to swarm all over Kid Irish here. But Kid Irish has a good pair of hands. He can handle himself. A left jab to the face, a right cross . . . combina- tions . . . he fights long . . . he moves in close . . . he ducks inside the big guy's wild swings . . . A short left to the ribs brings him down . . . a right uppercut snaps him up . . . It's right out of the book! He's a Joey Archer, this little kid, a Willie Pep, a Ken Buchanan of the streets. At last! a street fight worthy of the term! The bully keeps coming on, but he's . . . *getting his* . . . from the plucky little Irishman. It's a classic—

Just then a big Spanish guy about nineteen years old steps in from out of nowhere and stabs the Irish kid between the ribs with a knife and runs off, and that is all there is to that.

I'm telling you! That's New York! They took the kid into the emergency room, and he lived, but there it is! You can't win! Any man who voluntarily gets into a street fight in New York City is out of his hulking tree! I can tell you!

I'm only going over all this because thirty minutes ago, 8:15 P.M., I was out on First Avenue and Fiftieth Street trying to get a cab. Cold as hell, windy, and 8:15 p.m. it was, when cabs are scarce anyway. There's a man on the northwest corner already, a big man, a real custom-made Beekman Place burgher, by the looks of him. He's got it, the cab fever. He's been out here a long time. You can tell it. By now he is a good fifteen feet out into the intersection, straining this way and that, looking down First and along Fiftieth, trying to cover both possibilities. His eyes are lit up. Cab fever! He sees me coming. He looks at me like I'm a wild dog. I try to act like I'm just walking along the street. I happen to know the area. I know the only place you can get a cab around there at that hour is in front of La Toque Blanche restaurant on Fiftieth, near the corner, when a cab pulls up to let off people going to dinner. I duck into the doorway of the restaurant. Pretty soon a cab pulls up. I'm on top of it like a flash, hand on the door handle, before the people inside even have their money out, before the driver throws the meter off and lights up the light on top. But the big ace from Beekman Place has spotted it, too. He's roaring up. He bellies into me. I can't believe it. He's grappling for the door handle—

"No, you don't!" he says. "I've been waiting here half an hour!"

"Well, listen!" I'm saying. "Hey! Cut that out! I got here first!"

"Take your hand off the door, you asshole!"

Asshole!

"Who are you calling an asshole, you—"

But now the door is opening from the inside. There's an old couple inside. All they want to do is get inside La Toque Blanche and eat some gigot d'agneau and drink some wine. The woman is nearest the door and trying to get out. I can see her trying to creep her shoe and her spindly old calf out the door. She hasn't got a prayer, of course. This maniac and I are rousting and bellying each other against the door. Now the woman's husband is leaning across her to help her out. Her leg is stuck. It's not funny.

"Gentlemen!" he keeps saying. "Just a minute! Hear! Just a minute, you two!" and a lot of other stuff. And I swear, at that moment both the Beekman Place dude and I are about to turn on both of them. I can feel it. The one character all combatants hate worse than death or each other has arrived: *the spoilsport.* We're in a frenzy. With all this heaving and bellying we'll break the old doll's leg off for her. I can see it all coming. It's pure madness.

Only just then the big bastard I'm struggling with gets a brilliant idea. He runs over to the other side of the cab. I can still see him running. I can see his knees in the headlights. He brings his knees up high in fast little steps, the way they used to teach the fullback to do on the Deerfield "Junior Bulldogs" in 1951. Bango! He's into the cab from the other side. I'm left on the curb like a jerk. I catch all the outraged noise from the old guy and his wife as they limp into La Toque Blanche.

The cab pulls off and that great Melton-coat water buffalo sticks his head out of the window and yells: "You . . . asshole!"

And I'm left there on the curb in the dark, listening to myself gasp for breath in the void.

About the Author

TOM WOLFE is the author of a dozen books, among them such contemporary classics as *The Electric Kool-Aid Acid Test, The Right Stuff, The Bonfire of the Vanities,* and *A Man in Full.* A native of Richmond, Virginia, he earned his B.A. at Washington and Lee University and a Ph.D. in American studies at Yale. He lives in New York City.